Gaining A Yard

THE BUILDING OF BALTIMORE'S FOOTBALL STADIUM

Gaining A Yard

THE BUILDING OF BALTIMORE'S FOOTBALL STADIUM

WRITTEN BY
Jon Morgan

PHOTOGRAPHY BY
Doug Kapustin

PUBLISHED BY THE BALTIMORE SUN COMPANY, BALTIMORE, MARYLAND

THE BALTIMORE SUN

Published by
The Baltimore Sun
A Times-Mirror Co.
501 N. Calvert Street
Baltimore, MD 21278

Editor: Ray Frager
Picture Editor: Jim Preston
Design Editor: Joseph Hutchinson
Assistant Picture Editor: Jeffrey F. Bill
Designer: Jennifer Halbert

ISBN: 0-964-98197-1

Contents

February 27, 1997
*The sun begins to set on another workday for these construction workers.
As their surroundings attest, they have many more to go.*

February 27, 1997
*Workers prepare the form for
a grade beam as the stadium
supports begin to take shape.*

November 5, 1996
*(Opposite) Dave Garrett
works on preparing pilings.*

January 22, 1997
*(Preceding pages) One of the
huge cranes involved in the
project rises over the
construction site.*

Introduction

IN MANY RESPECTS, THEY WERE THE LEAST LIKE-
ly pair to commit the sporting world's crime of the century.

Art Modell had owned the Cleveland Browns since the days when the league consisted of only 14 franchises and mega-dollar television contracts were just a dream. He had grown up in Brooklyn, N.Y., a fan of the Dodgers, and knew first hand the the pain inflicted when a team jilted its city. He vowed many times never to do the same.

Baltimore had been a relative newcomer to profes-sional football, acquiring, then losing, then reacquiring the Colts in a comical series of events that began in 1947. But it caught up quickly and, in the crucial 1950s and 1960s, proved, like Cleveland, a hotbed that helped estab-lish the NFL as the Goliath of sports.

Then, on a slushy night in 1984, the city became the prototypical victim of sporting greed when the Colts moved unannounced to Indi-anapolis. Baltimore and Maryland moved quickly to solidify the city's major-league status, investing more than $200 million to build a new park for the Orioles and prepare for one for an NFL team — which it vowed to win the honest way, through league expansion, not larceny.

But this old-line city and old-guard owner did the un-thinkable in 1995. Spurred by what it perceived as slights at the hands of the arrogant league — which bypassed Baltimore in its 1993 expansion in favor of a pair of Sun Belt upstarts — the city cast aside its high-minded rhetoric and went on the prowl. With $200 million in pre-approved stadium financing on hand and the downtown land already cleared and set aside, Baltimore dangled the prospect of a publicly built palace in front of franchises from Oakland to Tampa.

No owner could ignore the siren's call, not even Art Modell. He was playing in a relic of a stadium and falling fast behind more junior owners luxuriating in new parks. The economic foundations of the sport, shaken by a new labor agreement with its players, now favored these own-ers, enriched as they were by millions of dollars flowing from their corporate skyboxes, premium club seat sec-tions and boutique concessions.

Modell had spent years trying to get a new or renovat-ed stadium in Cleveland, a city that in every other respect had been legendarily supportive of him and his franchise. But fate, and his own strategy, was not kind to his effort.

November 5, 1996

Nightfall doesn't mean work stops. This crew is setting pilings in preparation for the stadium's foundation.

13

He watched from the sidewalk as magnificent new facilities went up downtown for the American League Indians and NBA Cavaliers — projects he supported.

When his turn came, it seemed the money had run out. The Indians and Cavaliers projects had run badly over budget and an unrelated county bond crisis sapped the political energy to fund his job. Deadlines set by the mayor came and went, and Modell's team, burdened by debt piled up in an attempt to get to the Super Bowl, languished on and off the field.

Feeling betrayed, he commenced a series of meetings with Maryland officials that culminated in one of the best deals in sports. Maryland would build him the best stadium that money could buy and let him keep all the revenues that ensued — from every beer sale, every ticket sold and every stadium advertisement. As rent, the state would collect a ticket tax and Modell would reimburse the state for the $4 million or so it would cost each year to run the place.

Modell and his team would even be allowed to book concerts, college games and other events at the stadium and split the profits with the state.

It was, like similar deals being struck with other major-league teams around the country, including the Orioles a few years before, breathtakingly lucrative, and transformed overnight the fortunes of Modell and his franchise.

But it would also stain forever the legacy of the owner and the city. It seemed sure, at least in the short run, to keep Modell out of the Hall of Fame, for which he had been nominated in 1995. He was forever banished from Cleveland, his home of 35 years.

And for Baltimore, it meant the city could no longer portray itself as a virtuous victim of sporting greed.

But it was back in the NFL. And it was showcasing a stadium that very well may set a new standard for the sport, just as Oriole Park had done so for baseball.

August 6, 1997
A nosebleed seat? Ironworker Jimmy Edwards climbs among the reinforcement bars at the top of what will be the column on the south side of the stadium.

October 4, 1996
A backhoe excavates the ground at the site of the Ravens stadium with the BGE storage tanks in South Baltimore in the background.

15

August 6, 1997
He could go all the way... A worker is at about what will the 50-yard line while hauling material.

February 27, 1997
Paul Balton (left) and Charles Jordan, plumbers for J.W. Parker, review plans.

February 27, 1997
*High on a platform, Elijah Jones
and Allen Smith of Clark
Construction install a shoe jack
in preparation for a form pour.*

November 5, 1996
*A welder works on connecting
metal tubing for pilings with the
background lighted by a sign for
the doomed Hammerjacks club.*

January 22, 1997
*(Following pages) A worker
stands amid the concrete forms
of the stadium's foundation. The
receding sunlight transforms the
scene into an alien landscape.*

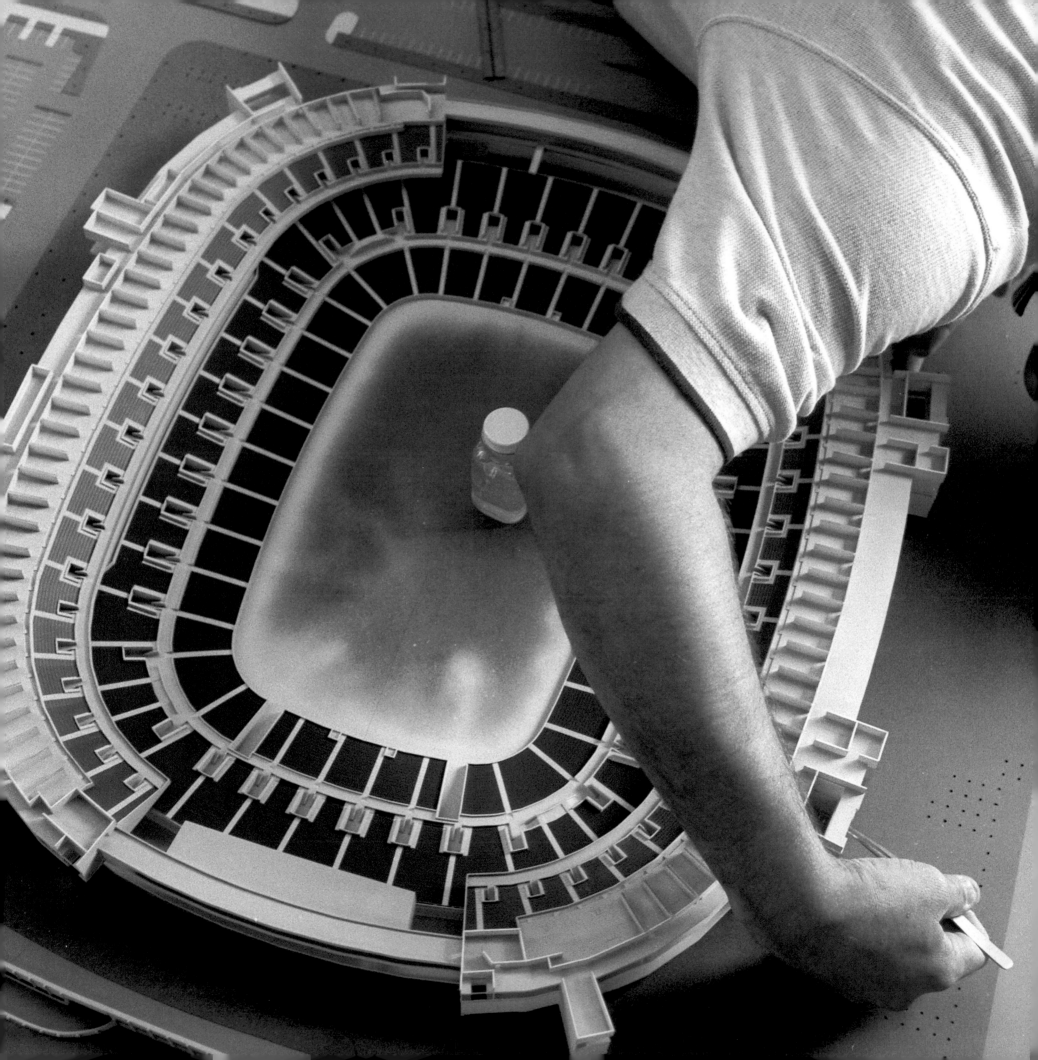

NFL stadiums:
a whole new game

APRIL 27, 1997 — WHEN THE DESIGN-ers set out to create Oriole Park, it was obvious where they needed to look for inspiration: Chicago's ivy-ringed Wrigley Field, Boston's quirky Fenway Park, Kansas City's clean and efficient Kauffman Stadium.

But where to find spiritual guidance for football, the sport of gargantuan, concrete ovals?

That is a challenge for the people building the Ravens stadium and other National Football League fields now in the works. For a league that has achieved a breathtaking dominance of American sports, the NFL has so far failed to open a single soul-stirring field.

Oh, there are stadiums with heritage and character. Chicago's Soldier Field has its lakefront location and handsome exterior flourishes. Giants Stadium in New Jersey's Meadowlands moves people in and out rapidly and is considered well-engineered, though visually unremarkable.

Jack Murphy Stadium in San Diego won design awards and boasts some thoughtful features and innovative finishes. The Carolina Panthers' new home has been well-received, but most of its applause has been for large and easy-to-find restrooms. Hardly the stuff of *Architectural Digest* centerfolds.

There is some nostalgia for college stadiums, such as the University of Pennsylvania's Franklin Field in Philadelphia, which are aesthetically and historically significant.

June 30, 1998
In Kansas City, Mo., Peter Friederich puts in tiny details of a stadium model, the third one he's done and the one that will stay in the offices of the stadium architects, HOK Sports Facilities Group.

23

The recently demolished Yale Bowl in New Haven, Conn., was also well-regarded.

"But none of them are especially revered," acknowledges Gordon Wood, a vice president of Ellerbe Becket in Kansas City, Mo., a major architectural firm active in stadium design. Fact is, when it comes to stadium design, football — especially the NFL — is dull, dull, dull.

The reasons are both subtle and obvious. Size is a big part. Baseball stadiums tend to run small, a relatively cozy 45,000 seats or so. This affords designers more flexibility in laying out a seating plan. Packing 70,000 seats into a football stadium requires the orderly use of almost every square inch, eliminating the gaps and angles that can give a park character.

The sheer bulk of a football stadium also defies a tidy integration with the cityscape, a la Camden Yards.

"Unfortunately, football stadiums are such immense beasts that they can't fit into their cities ... because of their size and shape and parking requirements, they're not easily assimilated," said John Pastier, an architectural critic and stadium consultant from Seattle.

A bigger size means a bigger price tag, too. Less money is left over for luxuries and extras that can make a stadium unique.

The shape of the field also presents limitations. Baseball is played on a diamond, but several basic dimensions, such as the distance from home plate to the outfield walls, are not standard. This gives designers the opportunity to shorten, say, the right-field line and compensate with a towering wall — as was done at Oriole Park.

By contrast, there are only so many ways to array seats around a rectangular gridiron.

"Once you get past the rectangular field, you can do what you want, but the tendency is to get people as close to the action as you can," Wood said. "What's the benefit to the fan if you put in nooks and crannies and it moves the fan away from the field?"

Also, the relationship between the fan and the game is different. Baseball's best seats are close to the players, at field level. The start-and-stop nature of the play, and the temperate summer weather, encourage fans to meander through concourses and linger in the stadium.

"In Baltimore, a trip to Camden Yards is a very complex experience, and the game is only one part of it. The culture of football is much different than the culture of baseball, which leads to very different stadiums," Pastier said.

The most coveted football seats are dead-center, well above the field so plays can be seen unfolding and players on the sideline don't obstruct the view.

"One thing you want for football is a sense that the crowd is right on top of you

June 19, 1997

Ed Lowery checks supports with a level in preparation for I-beam placement.

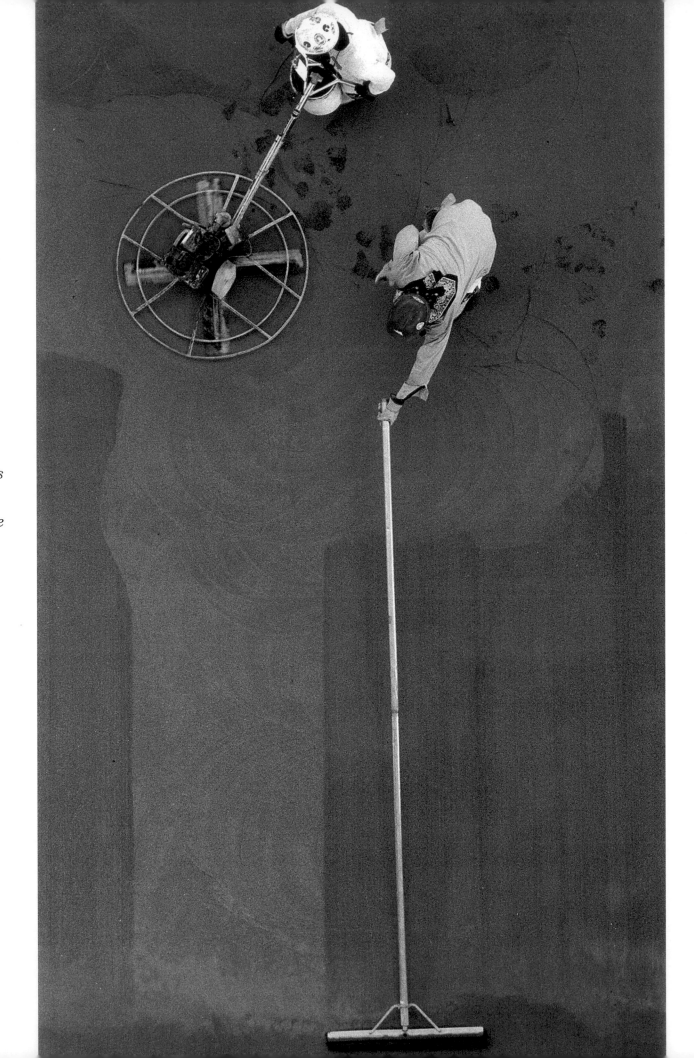

June 19, 1997
Concrete finishers Jerome Madison (left) and Louis Allen are in on the ground floor, taking care of a section on the stadium's main level.

and into the game," he said. "Baseball is a reflective game."

The rapid action of football also has structural implications: fans tend to surge to the concessions and washrooms at the same time, in three massive waves at the start, middle and end of the game.

There's also the relative youth of the sport. The NFL has been around since the 1920s, but it didn't emerge as a major league until the 1960s. It would be disingenuous for a football stadium to evoke nostalgia in the same way that Oriole Park made use of 19th-century baseball touches.

This has practical implications, too. Communities weren't investing in football stadiums in the first half of the century, when baseball and boxing were king. In those years, NFL teams were shoehorned into baseball parks. Or plopped into massive, round coliseums built for Olympic track and field competition, world fairs and other events.

For a while in the 1970s, a slew of ugly, "multipurpose" stadiums popped up around the country, designed to accommodate both baseball and football. These left fans and team owners in both sports dissatisfied.

"The whole idea of two-sport stadiums is an exercise in trying to square the circle — you'll never get it," Pastier said.

It's only been recently that the NFL has amassed the economic and political clout to demand its own, single-purpose parks. An unprecedented wave of stadium construction is under way, driven largely by changes in the financial underpinnings of the sport, and the desire for more revenue from luxury seating and concessions. This has given designers a new opportunity to focus solely on football and to create a standard.

New or overhauled stadiums have recently opened in Charlotte, N.C., and Jacksonville, Fla. Others are being built in Landover, Md., Baltimore and Cleveland. Plans are under way for more in Cincinnati, Seattle, Denver, Chicago, Detroit and Tampa, Fla.

Will the designers rise to the challenge? There is reason for hope, but whether anyone has struck upon a formula that will finally give football its own Wrigley Field — or Oriole Park at Camden Yards — remains to be seen.

"I think everybody is out there looking for the unique images and design — everyone would like to do it," said Wood. "There has been some discussion of trying to create unique seating areas people can take pride in."

Ravens stadium, for example. Its upper deck is going to be built in four sections, with the two end zones floating on their own, tucked in closer to the field. The open "notched" corners will provide a glimpse of the outer skyline, and a welcome break from the NFL's boring oval.

Cleveland's new stadium is also being built lopsided, with the upper deck higher along one sideline than the other, so fans on the north side can peer over those on the opposing side and see downtown. In homage to the former Cleveland Stadium's famed "dawg pound" rooting section, the eastern end zone will be distinct from the rest of the stadium, cut off with giant slots that will afford a view of nearby lakefront attractions.

In Cincinnati, the Bengals' stadium plan calls for perhaps the boldest shape of all. Along the sidelines, the upper decks will bulge in the middle and thin out at the ends — packing more seats in the middle of the field, where fans want to be. The end-zone sections will be separate, asymmetrical and modernistic. Seen from the field, the end-zone decks will be shaped like curved wedges, taller at one end than the other.

An asymmetrical bowl is not a new idea. College stadiums have routinely been built this way, generally because funding is unpredictable and stadiums add upper decks in fits, often only on the side that faces the sun. The University of Maryland's Byrd Stadium, for example. But making it work in the context of the NFL's mammoth capacity and economic demands will be tricky.

"You have to build them to accommodate the customer. The sightlines are what is important," said Robert Leffler, a local sports marketing executive and amateur stadium historian.

August 5, 1997
Ironworkers carry reinforcing
mesh to be embedded in concrete.

February 27, 1997
With the late afternoon sun throwing his shadow against a wall, plumber Gus Coleman sets up a transit to check on pipe elevations.

August 22, 1997
A welder is obscured by the concrete decking, but his task is illuminated during the third shift.

June 19, 1997
(Preceding pages) Near what will be the southwest entrance of the stadium, a worker is reflected in a pool of water from the previous day's showers.

June 19, 1997
(Following pages) A view from the top of crane No. 1 looking southwest.

Taxpayers fill bill for NFL stadiums

SEPTEMBER 14, 1997 — THE WASHINGTON REDSKINS today unveil a stadium that is remarkable not for its architecture, but for who paid the architect. The team becomes one of only four NFL franchises to play in a stadium constructed largely with the club's money.

As with most private stadium projects, the Redskins received significant government aid, but less than the norm in a league growing saturated with publicly financed palaces.

All of which raises the question: Why doesn't every team build its stadium?

Experts say NFL teams could, if forced to, pay for their stadiums the way most private companies provide their own offices and factories. But with the demand for franchises greater than the supply, communities stand ready to pay. And team owners stand ready to accept.

"Any of these teams could do it. They make money. The question is: Why do it if someone else is willing to?" said Allen Sanderson, an economics professor at the University of Chicago and frequent critic of public financing of stadiums.

"It's just like you can buy your own car, but if you can get someone else to do it, you'd be a fool," he said.

The NFL and its teams prefer to view the projects as "public-private partnerships" in which both sides prosper. The teams obtain modern venues necessary to keep revenue growing, and the cities receive taxes and other benefits from having a major-league team.

Baltimore felt the price worth paying: The $220 million stadium now under construction downtown for the Ravens is being built and financed by the state, although the team will contribute the equivalent of about $12 million toward construction.

"It's very difficult to structure a stadium deal that does not have a public component to it," said Roger Goodell, the NFL's senior vice president of league and football development.

Outdoor football stadiums do not attract many cash-making bookings other than NFL games and a handful of mega-concerts, religious revivals and other events. As a result, it is hard to make money on them the way you can with, say, an indoor arena — many of which are privately developed.

Could all-private financing be arranged? "I suppose it's possible," Goodell said. But with no taxpayer assistance,

July 8, 1997

With a crane towering behind him, Jerome Madison finishes concrete on stadium decking.

the financial burden would fall harder onto the other players: the fans, through ticket prices and seat licenses, and the team, by diverting money away from player salaries and into interest payments.

Cutting off the NFL from its taxpayer/stadium lifeline would also hurt it in the competition for fans and corporate support in cities with new, publicly financed baseball stadiums or arenas.

Even in celebrated cases such as the Redskins, the public role is large. Taxpayers put up $70.5 million for land, sewer lines, highway interchanges and other "infrastructure" necessary to move the Redskins to Landover, five miles from their old location in Washington.

But the $180 million construction budget was financed entirely by private sources. The giant Japanese-based Sumitomo Bank Ltd. and NationsBank of Charlotte, N.C., headed a consortium of four lenders that provided $155 million in loans. Put up as collateral was the stadium and its anticipated revenues, especially from its high concentration of pricey skyboxes and luxury seats.

Team owner Jack Kent Cooke, who died earlier this year, put up the other $20 million as equity. Years earlier, Cooke had also privately financed the Forum in suburban Los Angeles for the use of the NBA Lakers and NHL Kings, which he then owned. Both the Forum and Jack Kent Cooke Stadium were built in record time for the notoriously impatient team owner.

"Mr. Cooke did not want to have to ask the citizens of these communities to pay for his stadium. He felt this was something he could finance and build on his own and do it quicker and have control over the project," said Martin Klepper, an attorney with Skadden, Arps, Slate, Meagher & Flom in Washington, who represented Sumitomo and NationsBank in the deal. Klepper, who has negotiated similar deals for stadiums and arenas across the country, said most NFL teams probably could finance their stadiums unless they are burdened by debt, operating losses or other problems.

It's too soon to declare a trend, but private money has

sneaked into a few stadium deals around the country. Several arenas, such as the MCI Center in Washington and United Center in Chicago, have been privately developed, due in a large part to the economic usefulness of indoor arenas.

The San Francisco Giants are privately developing a new park, using a seat-license program untested in baseball. Even the mostly public football stadiums going up in Cleveland, Baltimore and Cincinnati have large team contributions. However, some of these contributions, when coupled with nearly rent-free leases, are a poor substitute for municipalities that once depended on a team's annual rent to pay off stadium bonds.

Other "private" stadiums benefited from public largess. The land under the Carolina Panthers' $190 million stadium in Charlotte, N.C., was bought and cleared at public expense — a jail and nursing home had to be relocated — and a parking garage was constructed nearby for the Panthers. Fans plunked down more than $130 million in season-ticket fees, called permanent seat licenses, to help finance the job.

When the late Dolphins owner Joe Robbie was turned down in two stadium-funding referendums, he went ahead and built a multisport stadium, now known as Pro Player Stadium, in 1988 in Dade County, Fla. He financed the $115 million with what was then a new wrinkle: club seats — extra-wide, luxury accommodations that required an annual rental fee on top of a season-ticket charge.

But the public helped, too. Tax-exempt bonds were issued, saving the team tens of millions of dollars in interest. The

September 26, 1997
(Above) This ramp will bring fans to and from their seats, but, on this day, it's a worker's path.

August 6, 1997
This entrance carries equipment inside the stadium, but the view eventually will be what football players see just before entering the field.

land was donated by a developer in a swap that enhanced the value of adjacent property.

The New England Patriots' stadium in Foxboro, Mass., was built in 1971 with $6 million raised through a real estate trust — an investment vehicle similar to a mutual fund. The team now says the stadium is inadequate and wants public financing for a new one.

The Carolina deal, in particular, shows that private financing should work, said Tom H. Regan, assistant professor of sports business at the University of South Carolina. The Panthers privately raised the money despite playing in a small market and taking on the $140 million expansion fee and onerous financial terms imposed by the NFL on its expansion franchises in 1993.

"If the Carolina Panthers can make it go with the burden they have, by God anyone can," Regan said.

Stadium building is not cheap. Principal and interest payments on a $200 million project would add up to $24 million for 15 years. A team would get an immediate tax benefit by "depreciating" the facility on its books, an accounting procedure that would shield about $7 million a year from taxes, Regan said.

More importantly, a team would enjoy a substantial burst of revenue from the luxury seating, corporate sponsorships, higher ticket prices and costlier concessions. Some new stadiums can generate $40 million or more of this kind of revenue.

The Ravens, for example, are selling 100 skyboxes and 7,900 club seats, which will bring in about $25 million a year, minus a few million given to the visiting teams.

The Redskins packed even more luxury into their new stadium: 15,000 club seats and 200 skyboxes.

James Bailey, the Ravens' executive vice president/legal and administration, said the Baltimore market would not have supported as many luxury seats, making a privately financed deal here less viable. Also, the franchise, formerly the Cleveland Browns, was burdened with debt and the costs of operating the old and uneconomical Cleveland Stadium, he said.

"In our case, certainly, it wouldn't work," Bailey said.

July 8, 1997
Steel walkways sit ready for concrete pours.

June 19, 1997
(Following pages) Gary Eby (center) guides a 33,000-pound concrete form into place.

January 9, 1998

(Above and opposite) Fans and VIPs gather to watch the topping-off ceremony. A light tower, marking the highest point of the stadium, is put into place.

August 27, 1997

(Preceding pages) Cranes watch over the stadium at night.

September 26, 1997

(Following pages) The view from a construction crane takes in the harbor and far beyond.

Ravens stadium is big, big deal

JANUARY 9, 1998 — TO UNDERSTAND JUST HOW BIG the Ravens' new downtown stadium is, consider that the Titanic, if dry-docked at Camden Yards, would be a mere 40 feet longer than the stadium and about only one-fifth its width.

The ship's funnel smokestacks would reach roughly to the height of the top of the stadium's uppermost light towers, the first of which will be installed in a "topping off" ceremony today.

Big? You could lay Baltimore's World Trade Center on its side along the 50-yard line and it would fit easily within the stadium's outline. You could hang the world's largest creature, a blue whale, from its tail off the top of the lights, and its head wouldn't come close to scraping the sidewalk below.

March 31, 1998

The field area is still covered by construction equipment, but the stadium very much resembles a place for football.

It is, in short, one of the biggest buildings ever erected in the state — 165 feet at its tallest point — dwarfing the nearby Oriole Park and surprising passers-by with its bulk.

"It's just huge. It reminds me of that movie 'Independence Day,' where everyone comes out in the morning and there's a huge spaceship hovering over the city. It just kind of hovers out there on Russell Street," said Bonnie O'Donnell, a receptionist for a company near the stadium.

Architects and community leaders have long expressed concern about the size of the building, because it serves as a "gateway" structure. It's the first thing many people see as they drive into the city from the south, and it could easily overwhelm everything for blocks around.

It also had a tough standard to live up to: Oriole Park won plaudits for its easy integration into its residential setting. "I think everybody was probably always concerned with the size of the thing. People had a fear about how it would fit into the neighborhood," said architect Peter Fillat of Beatty Harvey Fillat in Baltimore.

Fillat, active in the Urban Design Committee of Baltimore's American Institute of Architects chapter, was publicly critical of the stadium's early designs. But he likes what he sees rising out of the ground, and says the designers have done an effective job managing the project's visual scale.

"It's certainly a massive building. But it's a nice distance from the other stadium and downtown. I think it works. It bespeaks the character of a big-league city," Fillat said.

49

October 22, 1997
Structural steel rises above the seating bowl near Russell Street.

August 22, 1997
It's quitting time for this worker as he heads down a starkly lighted main concourse.

Designers felt less of a need to reduce scale on the industrial, southern end of Camden Yards than their counterparts did when building Oriole Park in a more residential area a few blocks north.

Besides, there was not much that could be done. It's just a big building — much bigger in capacity and square footage than Oriole Park. It will seat 69,000 people to the baseball park's 47,000.

That means more concession stands, more washrooms, more everything.

And it sits on land that slopes down to the Middle Branch of the Patapsco River, just 1,000 feet away. That means the water table is closer to the surface, so its playing field couldn't be sunk much deeper into the ground than Oriole Park's was or else it wouldn't drain properly.

That forces the rest of the stadium up higher.

"We could only go down so far, so it was up," said Bruce Hoffman, executive director of the Maryland Stadium Authority. "I was worried for a year that it was too big. I don't think it is now. I think it's a nice building."

A few functional factors, besides the capacity demands of football, also have contributed to the stadium's immense dimensions. Designers double-decked the 108 skyboxes to give them all sideline views. Early versions of the stadium called for a single deck of boxes rimming the field between the upper and lower decks.

The result: The top of the upper deck of the Ravens' stadium is 134 feet off the ground, and the lights add another 31 feet to that, pushing the entire structure up 165 feet. On the ground, the stadium is 844 feet by 438 feet. By contrast, Oriole Park's upper deck reaches about 85 feet into the air and its light towers about 140 feet up.

Even though both fields are sunk about 20 feet into the ground, Ravens players will be about nine feet lower than the Orioles relative to sea level because of the slope of the ground and the lower elevations at the Ravens' stadium.

Scale was a big concern at Oriole Park, according to a designer active on that project.

"We tried to make it more diminutive in size, and we tried some tricks of the eye to make it seem smaller," said Janet Marie Smith, who worked on Oriole Park and is now working on sports facilities in Atlanta for the Turner organization.

For example, the brick exterior of Oriole Park ends about 55 feet off the ground, giving the illusion of a building that is smaller than it really is. The rest of the superstructure is steel and concrete, providing a visual break.

Ravens stadium designers are aware of the issue of size, but don't believe it is as important a factor as it was with Oriole Park, said Heidi Edwards, a design consultant working for the football team.

"It's a different setting up there, and they had a lower scale context to work with. Our immediate context is much more warehouse-y and elevated roads. There's very

little to really overpower in the immediate vicinity," Edwards said.

The nearest buildings are industrial structures that may or may not be there in coming decades, unlike the distinctive Camden warehouse that was carefully incorporated into Oriole Park's design and kept its scale low, she said.

Some Ravens design elements have had the effect of minimizing scale, but were not expressly designed to do so, she said.

The upper deck, for example, is built in four separate sections, with gaps at the corners. This gives fans on the inside a view out, and also breaks up the crown of the stadium's exterior, she said.

"There was definitely attention paid to scale, but the building was never going to be as small as Oriole Park," Edwards said.

Smith, the Oriole Park veteran, said she is pleased with what she has seen so far but is reserving judgment on how it will turn out.

"I think the scale of it, which seems imposing now, will, if they continue with the same attention to detail I see now, be manageable," she said. "I think it's too early to pass judgment on whether it works at that site."

January 7, 1998
Gary Kline cuts crane loops off precast seating sections.

September 26, 1997
No permanent seat license is needed yet for ironworker Otto Weber, sitting in the upper level.

53

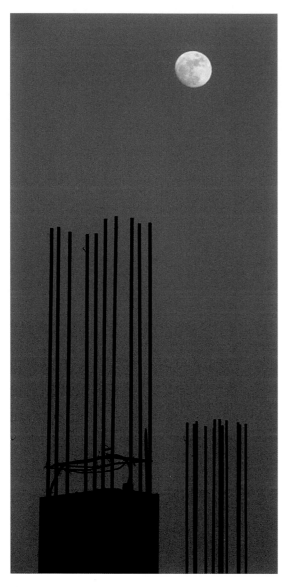

January 22, 1997
Newly formed concrete columns point at the moon.

April 14, 1998
Carpenter Homer Manning drills two holes at a time on the north side of the lower deck, preparing it for installation of seating hardware.

Concrete costs lead to stadium overrun

AUGUST 16, 1997 — THE CONTRACTOR POURING concrete for the Ravens' new stadium promised a year ago to negotiate a cap on the cost with the Maryland Stadium Authority, but the sides never reached agreement and the state is facing more than $10 million in overruns.

The contractor, Clark Construction Group, is to receive a guaranteed fee of $2.5 million on the job, regardless of the final costs. But its bills to the state — now running a third higher than anticipated — are largely responsible for pushing the cost of the stadium 10 percent above budget, to a projected $220 million.

"We are having some real heart-to-heart discussions with Clark," stadium authority Chairman John Moag said.

The Bethesda-based Clark, one of the nation's biggest construction firms, signed a contract with the stadium authority on August 16, 1996, to pour and form the concrete foundation, columns, ramps and other structural elements of the stadium. Clark, the only company to bid on the job, did so under a "fast-track" process: It agreed to receive a flat fee and would bill the state later for the cost of the work.

February 27, 1997
A concrete container moves into place for a foundation pour.

The stadium authority complained to Clark about its performance, which led to some personnel changes on the site earlier this year. Productivity and supervision were not as good as hoped for, and some work, including two big columns, had to be torn out and redone. Minutes of the weekly progress meetings of contractors reflect several references to Clark workers' crushing pipe with lifts and failing to complete sections of work on time.

Clark's work has improved in recent months, according to the stadium authority, which lists the productivity of the contractor as only one factor — along with design changes and a hot-running economy — responsible for the overruns.

"Early on, it was not good at the very beginning, but it is better now. They are ahead of schedule. We have a good working relationship with them. I think they are doing their best," stadium authority executive director Bruce Hoffman said.

Clark spokeswoman Louise Pulizzi said the company would not comment.

The fast-track bidding, common in hurry-up jobs like stadiums, allows the contractors to begin work before the final designs are completed.

57

April 8, 1998
James Williamson sets step forms for concrete on the lower level.

Clark estimated that the work would cost $30.8 million, and agreed to negotiate a "guaranteed maximum price" with the state, according to the contract and minutes of the September 4, 1996, Board of Public Works meeting.

Bid documents provided to the board, made up of the state governor, treasurer and comptroller, said the "cost of work is anticipated to be approximately $30.8 million."

But, despite months of negotiations, no guaranteed price was ever agreed to with Clark, and the stadium authority now estimates that the job may come in as high as $44 million. Hoffman said he hopes to keep it to $40 million through negotiation and redesign, if necessary.

This, along with an unexpectedly high bid for "precast" concrete seating decks, is the primary culprit in the stadium authority's surprise admission last month that the downtown stadium will likely cost $220 million.

The public's investment is still limited to $200 million; the team will cover the overruns, but largely through contributions it was required to make anyway. For example, $24 million in team contributions demanded by the General Assembly will now go toward paying overruns instead of retiring bonds or otherwise reimbursing the state for its $200 million investment.

Clark initially bid a lump-sum fee of $2.75 million for the job to cover overhead, profit and supervision, according to stadium authority documents. The authority negotiated the lump sum down to $2.5 million, with the chance for Clark to earn up to $500,000 in incentive bonuses for meeting certain performance standards.

The contract specified that a guaranteed price would be negotiated when the design was 50 percent complete. Stadium authority officials told the Board of Public Works last August that the designs should be half done, and the guaranteed price agreed to, by October 1996.

It wasn't.

The following March, Clark proposed a $35 million guaranteed maximum.

But weeks later, when the stadium authority attempted to accept the offer, Clark took the offer off the table, saying it could not do the work for $35 million.

"Early on, we would have loved a low number, but we didn't get one. They weren't going to sign a contract that would cause them to lose money," Hoffman said.

Given the stadium's aggressive timetable, replacing the structural concrete contractor — one of the biggest items in the project's budget — that late in the game would have been impossible.

State Treasurer Richard Dixon said he is not happy that the promised guaranteed price was not negotiated, and would be more skeptical of future contracts structured that way. But he accepted the stadium authority's explanation for the overruns.

"No one likes to hear about cost overruns, but occasionally they do occur," Dixon said.

April 14, 1998
*Outside the
stadium, Natala
Reves and Rogero
Melara build
concrete forms.*

59

Hoffman said the robust economy is largely to blame, although other major contracts negotiated at the same time and under similar fast-track procedures, for mechanical and electrical work, have remained within budget and under guaranteed prices negotiated with the contractors.

Concrete work is in high demand, and some companies have suffered a lack of productivity as they scramble to find qualified employees, Hoffman said.

"You've got people who are not the best; the best people may be at another job. The budget seems to go up," Hoffman said of the frenzied construction industry.

The Ravens' project has also experienced design changes that have required the addition of more steel reinforcement into the concrete than initially planned, driving up the costs.

Robert W. Dorsey, a professor of construction science at the University of Cincinnati, said fast-tracking big projects has become the norm. Ideally, it allows contractors and designers to work together to keep costs down and shaves months off the time it takes to complete a project.

The downside is that a contractor is locked in — and others excluded — before the price of the job is agreed to or the scope of the job even known.

The economy has created some spot shortages of trained workers and put pressure on other elements of construction, but those factors should be known far enough in advance to be worked into estimates, Dorsey said.

"Theoretically, it does affect the work because of supply and demand. But inflation has been held in check. I think it's valid to say there is a labor problem. You can get the bodies on site, but they may not be as trained as you like," he said.

Engineering News Record, a magazine that follows the construction industry, reported that the "construction cost index" was up 4.5 percent through the first six months of this year, driven largely by a spike in lumber costs. Construction-related wages nationwide are up 2.9 percent, structural steel 5 percent and cement 3.2 percent.

August 5, 1997
Clyde Gibbs uses rebar to ready a column for a concrete pour.

August 22, 1997
(Opposite) A precast seating section is put into place.

November 26, 1997
(Following pages) A year from now, that muddy floor will be a field and that structure filled with fans.

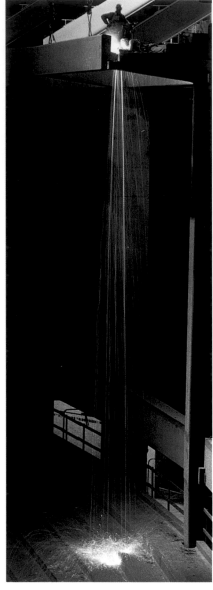

November 26, 1997
Chris Jeffries welds before a precast concrete beam goes into the upper deck.

December 13, 1997
Waterproofer Jim Brinson caulks joints in the upper-deck seating bowl.

April 14, 1998
(Following pages) It's not exactly like installing your rec room stereo system. Ed Grove (left) and Dale Klingelhofer of Enterprise Electric put in speakers on a light tower.

Scores courtesy of the space age

NOVEMBER 1, 1997 — FORGET SCRATCHY FIGHT songs booming from a tower of speakers and a black-and-white scoreboard endlessly flickering downs, points and timeouts remaining.

The $220 million Ravens stadium being built downtown is incorporating audio and video technology so cutting-edge that its planners say it will revolutionize the fan experience with animated graphics, multiple replay screens, computer-synchronized speakers — and perhaps even a Barry Levinson film short.

More than $10 million in specialized electronics will give controllers the ability to recreate the effect of a thundering squadron of jets swooping through the seating bowl, entering at one end zone and exiting at the opposite.

Fans cheering on a late-game drive will take their cues from sound effects so sophisticated they can mimic the roar of a locomotive circling the field, then reproduce with crystal clarity the guitar licks of the Rolling Stones.

July 14, 1998
From behind one of the scoreboards, light streams between slats in a rotating advertising board, which can accommodate three ads during a game.

"We think this will be the beginning of a revolution," said Eli Eisenberg, director of technical systems for the Maryland Stadium Authority.

The boards will be among the biggest in sports — 96 feet long and 24 feet high — and the first outdoor screens to use technology perfected only in the past few years.

Operators can, with the stroke of a few computer keys, dedicate the entire board to a high-fidelity video replay, then break the board up into 16 sections showing simultaneous live cuts of games going on around the league or out-of-town score updates.

"We will be the first to install it and the first to use it. We will be trailblazing," said Ravens executive vice president David Modell.

"What we are trying to do, as we are doing generally, is not to accept any of the preconceived notions of how fans have been entertained in the seating bowls," Modell said.

The Ravens have contacted Baltimore-born filmmaker Levinson to tap into his creativity on ways to use the new capabilities.

The key to the video system will be millions of "light-emitting diodes," each the size of a pencil eraser. Each diode contains a pair of silicon electrodes mounted on a sapphire and encased in a plastic shell. When an electrical

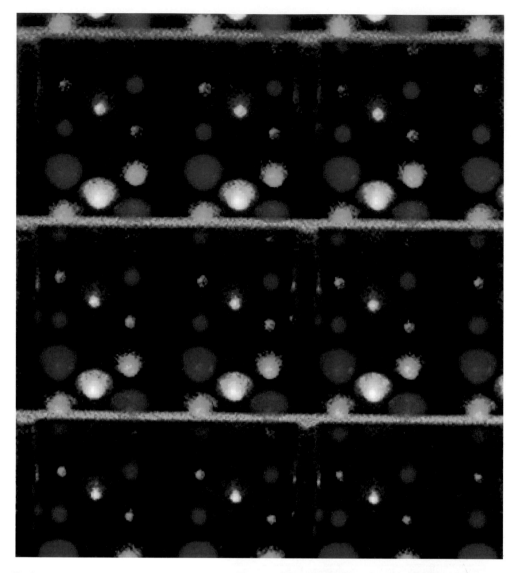

current is passed between the electrodes, a glow is created. Different hues are created by adding chemicals to the electrodes.

It is the same technology that has for years powered the familiar red glow of alarm clocks and digital watches. But recent advances — chiefly the creation in Japan of a chemical that makes the silicon electrodes give off a blue glow — has put red, blue and green LED's at a designer's disposal.

Clustered into "pixels," each LED can have its brightness turned up or down by a computer. The effect, when seen from a distance, is like an electronic pallet mixing paints to create different shades and colors.

SACO says the "SmartVision" boards it is building for the Ravens are capable of reproducing more than 16 million colors. At peak output — projecting an all-white screen — each board will consume up to 80,000 watts of power.

"It will be unique and, I think, unlike anything anyone has ever seen," said Fred Jalbout, president of SACO SmartVision Inc. of Montreal, the leader in the new, LED video board technology.

The Ravens' board will be the most important installation yet of the new technology, and SACO negotiated a stiff discount to get the job and show it off to potential customers. The purchase price for the two boards is listed as $8.7 million, but $2.3 million was waived as part of a "sponsorship credit" that came along with a skybox and other goodies. Of the remaining bill, the state will pay $5 million and the team the balance.

Jalbout predicts it will render obsolete better-known competitors, such as Sony's JumboTron, Mitsubishi's DiamondVision and Panasonic's Astrovision. Those boards operate on cathode-ray-tube technology, essentially an integrated network of television or color computer screens. They are costly, heavy and require a lot of electricity. Jalbout says his board will be cheaper to operate, require less maintenance, last longer and create more lifelike pictures.

Competitors aren't so sure. They say the LED's won't work as well in daylight as CRT boards and that its reliability is untested. That's why the stadium authority and the Ravens spent months researching the purchase.

"You don't want to be the first with new technology or the last with old technology. We looked into this very carefully," said Bruce Hoffman, executive director of the stadium authority.

Among the tests: several visits to concerts by the rock group U2, whose shows feature the first giant LED board built by SACO, and a special side-by-side comparison this summer at Oriole Park with the Sony JumboTron CRT board and a SmartVision test panel.

"We think this display system is going to rewrite the way people look at in-stadium entertainment," Eisenberg said.

July 14, 1998

Up close (above), the LED scoreboard takes on a hive-like look. Behind that hive (right), is a mass of wires and circuit boards. And the result (opposite) is a picture probably unlike any that fans have seen before in a stadium.

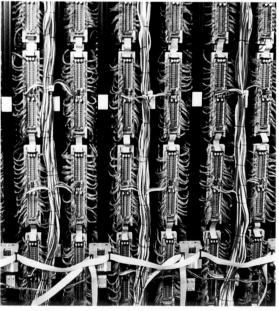

Biggest and brightest

The new SmartVision video display screen at the Ravens stadium consists of 9 million light emitting diodes, about the size of a Tic Tac. These require less power than other types of scoreboards, which allows them to be larger, longer-lasting and 60 percent brighter.

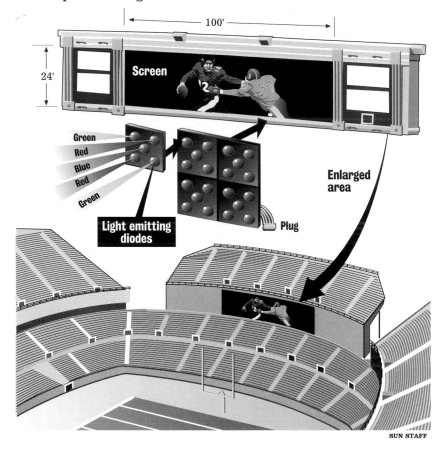

100'

24'

Screen

Green
Red
Blue
Red
Green

Light emitting diodes

Enlarged area

Plug

SUN STAFF

Similarly, a network of 1,894 custom-built speakers mounted throughout the stadium will create a fidelity and special effects capability new to the NFL. Unlike conventional systems, which concentrate speakers in one location and result in unwanted drifting and acoustical distortion, the Ravens' stadium will put a speaker within 144 feet of each fan's head.

Controlled by computers and driven by up to 300,000 watts of power, these speakers can be tuned to the contours of the stadium. In fact, the stadium authority hopes to invite 30,000 or so close friends over before the stadium opens to have them sit in stands and test the aim and balance of the system. The fans affect the acoustics, as the stadium authority has learned at Oriole Park, where a similar "distributed" sound system is also in place.

The audio and video system will be operated by a crew of up to 20 working out of a command center at the stadium on game day. Although capable of playing videotapes and compact discs, the system will rely mostly on music and images digitally encoded on a computer hard drive. Organists need not apply.

There will also be traditional modes of entertainment. A pair of cheerleading units is planned, one dance-oriented and the other traditional collegiate style. And the inimitable Colts Marching Band will be renamed the Ravens Marching Band, continuing a musical tradition that began 50 years ago.

The team also is exploring the reduction of visual "clutter" in the stadium by putting advertisements on flexible, backlit screens mounted on rollers. Several times throughout a game, the screens can be advanced or rewound, changing the ad. These rotating panels may be mounted on either side of the scoreboards and on the fascia along the sidelines.

This way, the team can offer a sponsor — for a handsome price — a "moment of advertising exclusivity" throughout the interior of the stadium.

These panels could also be synchronized with the video boards and sound-system to create eye-catching effects.

"I guarantee it will be spectacular," Modell said.

July 14, 1998
A view of the stadium from over the mixing board in the control room.

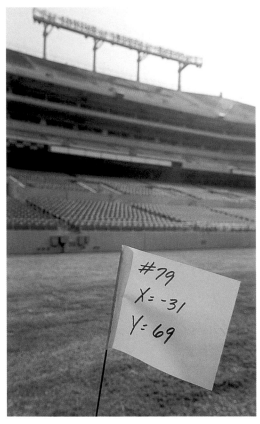

June 26, 1998
Flags mark coordinates on the field during the aiming of lights.

June 18, 1998
Electrician John Newman of Enterprise Electric takes care of wiring in a light tower that well may offer literally a bird's-eye view.

July 14, 1998
(Following pages) One of the state-of-the-art video screens that dominate each end zone.

April 8, 1998
*Franklin Smith begins the
grading work on what will be
the stadium playing field.*

April 23, 1998
*(Opposite) Cleat marks in grass
soon will replace bulldozer
tracks in dirt in this area.*

June 2, 1998
*(Preceding pages) A mixture of
sand and topsoil is spread over
the tubing that will control the
field temperature. Jimmy
Juergens (left) of the Ravens
grounds crew works with Tim
Houston and Mike Shumar of
S.W. Franks, the field
construction contractor, while
Mark Kelly drives the grader.*

When Ravens move downtown, they'll take their turf with them

FEBRUARY 25, 1998 — THE RAVENS HAVE BEGUN A project that a weekend gardener could only marvel at: picking up and relocating a lawn as big as, well, a football field.

The NFL team is carefully peeling its field at Memorial Stadium and laying it on an adjacent parking lot. There it will remain, secured by a chain-link fence and babied by groundskeepers, until June, when it will be rolled up again and trucked to the new stadium at Camden Yards.

"We're the first ones to relocate a field like this," said Ravens head groundskeeper Vince Patterozzi.

The reason for all this effort is the unique, costly nature of the field. The Ravens were the first pro team to use SportGrass, a patented system of growing natural grass through a synthetic-fabric base. The idea is to combine the strength and resilience of fake turf with the cushion of the real thing. The field was provided by the McLean, Va.-based Sport-Grass at a discount so it might attract other customers. Leaving it behind and installing a new field would cost more than $1 million. It is five times as expensive as regular turf.

Patterozzi said the

May 29, 1998

Mac Ensign and Mark Kelly lay the last section of 40 miles of tubing for under the playing field. Heating and temperature sensors are designed to keep the turf in optimum condition, even in cold weather.

Ravens have been pleased with their faux sod, and players — who blame artificial turf for knee and other injuries — have been enthusiastic.

The unusual moving project began last week when a "harvesting machine" began recutting the field into the original 42-inch-wide, 38-foot-long strips that came from a Florida sod farm in 1996. The strips were rolled up like giant toilet-paper rolls, taken to the parking lot and unrolled on the asphalt.

"We couldn't do this in the heat of July. But we've seen over the years that for a couple of months, you can put it on a hard surface like that," Patterozzi said.

The synthetic backing keeps the grass and soil together. Underneath is a sandy base covering a labyrinth of 38 miles of high-density plastic tubing, through which heated water is pumped to keep the field from freezing on cold days. This, too, is being dug up and will be installed at Camden Yards.

The transplanted grass — 70,000 square feet of it — will be watered and pampered in the parking lot until it is moved downtown. After a few weeks of settling, the field will be ready for the pitter-patter of offensive linemen's cleated feet.

Among other things, the relocation of the field means there is no turning back for the Ravens. The new stadium will have to open for the Aug. 8 exhibition.

"Unless we want to play in the parking lot," Patterozzi said.

June 12, 1998
The Ravens grounds crew and S.W.
Franks workers team to lay sod on the
field.

July 13, 1998
(Following pages) Less than a month
before the first exhibition game, grass
has taken root on the field.

Stadium no slave to fashion

MARCH 18, 1998 — IT TOOK EIGHT MONTHS AND more than 100 bricklayers, but the last of 1.2 million burgundy-colored bricks has been cemented into place at the Ravens stadium, giving the project its most distinctive visual signature.

Designers of the $220 million stadium hope the brick will both integrate the structure with nearby Oriole Park and give it a flourish that will be copied in other cities.

But at least for the time being, it will stand alone. Despite baseball's enthusiastic embrace of brick facades, the Ravens' is the first football stadium in decades to use the graceful, but pricey siding.

The reason? The high cost of laying brick accounts for some of the reluctance. But there is also a sense that the 19th-century motif doesn't mesh with a sport that came of age after the Beatles invaded America.

Concrete, glass, stone and steel — but no bricks — were used at new football parks in Charlotte, N.C.; Jacksonville, Fla.; Atlanta; and Landover. The same for planned stadiums in Tampa, Fla.; Nashville, Tenn.; Cincinnati; and Cleveland.

April 8, 1998

Around the arches on the south side of the stadium, Scott Weber washes off brick, whose presence is a link to football's past.

Seattle's new football stadium is still in the planning stage, and brick is a possibility — although a spokeswoman says the odds are less than 50-50. St. Louis accented its stadium with brick, but mainly used concrete.

Those involved with the Ravens' project think that's a shame. Recent football stadium design has tended to stress the newness of the sport and its emphasis on raw power over finesse.

But the game got its start in mostly brick college bowls around the country, some of which compare in age to the most venerated of baseball parks.

"There is a warmth to the brick, an almost collegiate atmosphere. It harkens back to campuses," said Heidi Edwards, an architect and the Ravens stadium project manager.

It also imparts a welcoming texture difficult to duplicate with steel or other materials, she said. "It's tactile. People walk up and touch brick," she said.

Stadium consultant John Pastier of Seattle, who is not connected with the Ravens' project, said brick has not been used much in football stadiums because of the costs.

"Bricks are expensive. Not so much the material, but the labor. You've got to assemble all those tiny pieces," Pastier said.

The Ravens stadium masonry, including interior concrete blocks, has cost $8.9 million to buy and install.

Baseball stadium planners have been less impeded by costs because those parks are smaller and require fewer bricks — Oriole Park used almost half as many, 750,000 — and the buildings get more use.

A baseball team plays 81 home games to a football team's two exhibition and eight regular-season games.

"There's a need for greater economy of structure in a football stadium than a baseball stadium. A football stadium tends to be a bare-bones structure," Pastier said.

Much thought was put into the Ravens' bricks. A few sample walls, each a few feet tall, were constructed.

Team owner Art Modell and Maryland Stadium Authority officials reviewed the choices before settling on No. 154 Montgomery, made by Redland Inc.-Cushwa Plant of Williamsport, Md., the nation's oldest continuously operated brick factory.

Designers picked brick for the football stadium to both blend and contrast it with its acclaimed cousin to the north.

Oriole Park's red bricks matched the 19th-century rowhouses and the B&O warehouse in its neighborhood.

The Ravens' brick is a deeper, richer hue. Combined with the pewter-colored mortar, the masonry is suppose to reflect the industrial flavor of the southern end of Camden Yards.

The brick maker hopes Baltimore can spark a renaissance in brick facades in the NFL, as Oriole Park did in baseball.

The company supplied the bricks for Oriole Park and bid a lower per-brick price for the Ravens' job.

"We're glad to see this use for brick on a stadium. Camden Yards spawned brick stadiums in Texas, Coors Field and Jacobs Field. We think this may spawn brick football stadiums," said Joe Miles, mid-Atlantic sales manager for Redland.

The Cushwa plant made the Ravens' bricks of shale mined from the banks of the Potomac River.

The same plant has supplied much of the region's bricks over the past century, including Washington's Georgetown district, shipping the masonry by barge down the Chesapeake and Ohio Canal.

The technology is ancient. Brick making has been traced back 6,000 years. The Cushwa plant has modernized and computerized the seven-day process, using kilns that heat the shale up to 2,000 degrees.

October 22, 1997
Joe Carter lays a course of bricks. Under the right conditions, he can lay 900 a day -- almost a half-ton.

Bricklaying is also time-honored, a craft requiring both patience and productivity.

Charlie Smith, a brick foreman in charge of the Ravens' project for Baltimore/Banner Joint Venture, the masonry contractor for the job, said quality bricklayers

June 9, 1997
Bricks bearing the team's name, manufactured by Redland-Cushwa of Williamsport, Md., stand ready to be set during a "first brick" ceremony. The Ravens logo itself (above) can be found on various arches and columns.

are hard to find, even in a city as fond of brick as Baltimore.

"Some are natural, believe it or not. A bricklayer has to be of a certain temperament. He has to be able to move. His whole body has to move. He has to be able to produce," Smith says.

Joe Carter, one of the 120 bricklayers, foremen and assistants who worked on the Ravens stadium, agreed.

"As you get older, you learn to do the same amount with less work. You can work easier if you work smarter," said Carter, 58.

Interviewed at the height of the job, Carter was a portrait of efficiency. No movement was wasted, no energy expended without purpose.

With a battered trowel, he neatly scooped each dollop of mortar from a trough and laid it onto a row of just-stacked bricks. Then he coated one end of a brick and planted it in place. Then another. And another.

The work demands the gentlest of touches with the harshest of materials. Too much mortar and it will squish out the sides; too little and the line of bricks will dip and jump instead of flowing symmetrically.

"It's become a habit. You just keep moving. Some days, everything falls into place," he said.

He can lay 900 bricks a day — nearly a half-ton — if the weather cooperates and the design is simple.

And when he's done, he can point to a project that's likely to outlive him.

"Every time my wife and I drive around the city, I say I worked on that building," Carter said.

September 26, 1997
Brick mason Barbara Moore removes rubber spacers between brick in an archway.

Deep-seated effort matches fans, spots

DECEMBER 20, 1997 — THEY DON'T KNOW IT, BUT tens of thousands of Ravens fans are having their game-day futures into the next century decided in a cluttered series of cubicles at the team's downtown offices.

Workers there have begun the painstaking process of assigning seats at the new stadium to the people who ordered them over the past two years.

There are computers and special software to help, but meshing the labyrinth of seating "zones" with orders, keeping groups of friends together and accommodating physical disabilities and idiosyncratic preferences is a job done largely by hand.

It will take months.

"There is no fail-safe way of doing it, unless you invite everyone out there one at a time. From a time perspective, you can't do that," said Roy Sommerhof, Ravens director of ticket operations.

For one thing, the stadium keeps changing.

Architects continually update what they believe will be the seating layout, down to the specific number of 20- and 19-inch-wide seats (the short ones are thrown in sometimes to make a row fit). But if one of the massive, concrete seating bowl sections comes in a few inches long or short, or if an expansion joint expands more than anticipated, it could add or subtract a seat or two.

"Sometimes what architects and engineers tell you on paper and what gets built are two different things," Sommerhof said. "You can get plus or minus 1 percent or 2 percent in each section."

The precise number of seats won't be known until they are bolted down and team officials can go out and count all 69,000 one-by-one.

In the meantime, the downtown employees are making their best guess and fitting in fans according to four levels of priority, seven price levels and eight zones. Seats at the new stadium will cost $200 to $600 a season, and most will require a one-time season-ticket surcharge, called a permanent seat license, of $250 to $3,000 (not including skybox and club seats).

The employees have started in a small, upper-deck corner, to get a feel for the process. First step: Baker Koppelman, assistant director of ticket operations, goes over a blueprint with a yellow marker and blocks out seats likely

April 23, 1998
Before carpenters could begin installing the seats, rows of supports (being inspected by Rick Carper, preceding pages) had to be in place.

to have undesirable views, such as the rows immediately behind railings. These will be set aside for single-game sales or filled in for the last season-ticket orders.

Then he turns to a computer that has reduced each seat to a tiny "O" on a diagram of a section. Each O becomes an X on the computer screen as a fan is assigned a seat. Fed into the computer are the individual accounts, their preferences for seats and other pertinent data.

Fans are then sorted according to priority: first are the diehards who put down money for club seats as part of the city's 1993 drive to land an expansion franchise and left the money on account but opted not to get a club seat.

Next are the fans who put down money in 1993 but requested a refund when the city failed to win a team. Third are the people who bought season tickets in 1996 and fourth are the new buyers.

Each buyer was asked to specify an area in the stadium, called a zone, where he wanted to sit. For each zone, the computer will "randomize" the accounts within each priority level (except for new buyers, who will be prioritized according to date of purchase). Koppelman and his assistants then take them in order, by hand, and fill them in on the computer, making broad assumptions about seating desirability.

Within a zone, for example, it's assumed that the better seats start at the lowest row nearest midfield and go up vertically, one behind the other, up to a certain point. Then, common sense suggests, preferences would move back down a few rows, and out from the midsection.

"If you are not a detail person, you should not be in this business," Koppelman said.

About 2,000 ticket buyers wrote in special requests, such as a seat on an aisle or one on the sunny side or the Ravens' side of the stadium. The team tries to accommodate as many of these as it can, although restrictions may have the effect of pushing a fan's seats higher in the stadium.

Groups of fans are bunched together and fitted into the matrix of O's on the computer screen. Care is taken to keep aisles from dividing groups. Four or fewer tickets in a single account are usually assigned as four in a row.

Groups of six or more are generally seated one behind the other in rows of three each.

An assignment may change throughout the process as blocks of people are fit into the puzzle. The team employees refer frequently to the stadium blueprints to be sure it matches the computer.

After the first priority customers are slotted into their seats, the team moves on to the second, third and fourth priority.

About 150 disabled season-ticket buyers will be assigned "infill" seats around the stadium. These seats, which can be installed and removed for each game, are scattered around the first rows of various levels and price categories of the stadium. As many as 4,000 infill seats may be available in the stadium, and will also be used by the team for players' families, visiting teams, VIPs, single-game sales and other allotments.

The team figures it will take about 2 1/2 months to go through the whole stadium, assigning the seats. And even then there are likely to be revisions.

Fans, who already know which zone they have been slotted into, will be notified of their specific seats in late March.

The team recognizes the special pressures the seat licenses put on the seat selection. There won't be as many opportunities to upgrade as there are with regular season tickets. A fan will hold the rights to a specific seat or seats. They can be sold and traded, but unless the team establishes a clearinghouse to help with this (and it might), the ticket buyers will be on their own.

"This is a long-term thing," Sommerhof said. "They hope to pass this on to their children. It's very important to them. People have a passion for football and have an equal passion for where they sit."

As long as you get a seat in one of the zones you requested, there will be no refunds. In fact, fans won't find out their precise seat assignment until after they make their final payments.

"You're never going to make everyone happy," Koppelman said. "But as long as the customers feel they were treated fairly, we're OK."

June 25, 1998
Bill Salbeck puts in seats near the edge of the upper deck.

April 14, 1998
(Following pages) A lone carpenter works installing seats in west side of the upper-deck end zone.

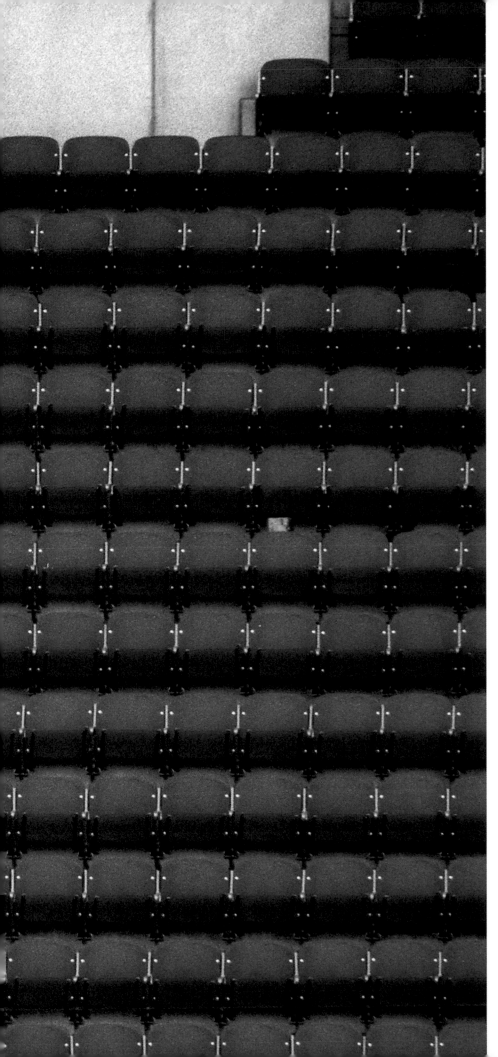

Seating at new stadium

The Ravens are assigning seats to fans who have purchased PSLs and season tickets. The new stadium is divided into zones.

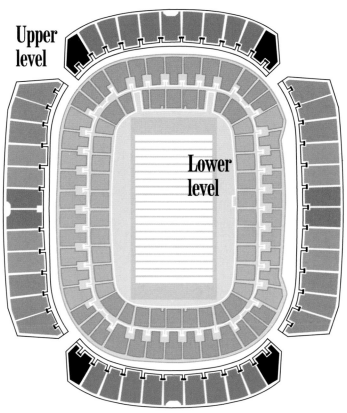

Upper level

Lower level

Zone key

▬ A zone	▬ B zone	▬ C zone	▬ D zone
▬ E zone	▬ F zone	▬ G zone	▬ H zone

Ravens seating

Zone (Location)	PSL	Season ticket	No. of seats *
A (Lower level midfield)	$3,000	$600	5,800
B (Lower level sideline)	$1,500	$500	9,000
C (Lower level end zone)	$750	$350	16,000
D (Upper level midfield)	$2,000	$550	2,500
E (Upper level sideline)	$1,000	$450	5,500
F (Upper level goal line)	$750	$350	7,900
G (Upper level end zone)	$500	$300	9,000
H (Upper level corner)	$250	$200	2,100

*Approximate
SOURCE: Baltimore Ravens

SHIRDELL MCDONALD : SUN STAFF

For $4.75M, stadium sitting pretty

MAY 21, 1997 — ITS CONTOURS ARE SLEEK, NEARLY aerodynamic. The acceleration may be a little disappointing, but it hugs the curves, promises Ripken-like durability and costs only about $70. That's without the optional cup holder.

After months of study and comparison — including an unscientific, sit-down marketing test — the seats have been selected for the Ravens' stadium. The Maryland Stadium Authority last week approved a $4.75 million contract with American Seating for 67,822 plastic and iron, spring-loaded chairs.

The custom-designed seats, made in Grand Rapids, Michigan, by the same firm that make Oriole Park's retro-style seats, will have a purple seat and back and metallic gray frames. The purple will complement the Ravens' uniforms; the gray will do the same for the pewter-colored structural steel in the stadium.

The seats and competing models had to survive rigorous testing at the Maryland Stadium Authority's offices. Five finalist seats were mounted on stands and lined up for employees and visitors to test-sit. Testers filled out forms, ranking the seats for comfort and appearance.

For denizens of Memorial Stadium's mish-mash of bench and narrow aluminum seats, the new digs will be a big upgrade. Upper- and lower-deck seats will be 19 inches wide; pricier club seats will be 21 inches across. An ergonomic design promises enhanced lower-back support.

Gravity will drive the seat bottom up when not in use, to drain off rain and provide access for cleaning crews. When a few extra inches are needed to make way for passing fans, the seat can be pushed back even farther against a spring mechanism.

June 26, 1998
Grant Wedding, whose company is in charge of installing the seating, checks over his handiwork, which gets a powerwashing from Nathaniel Gantt (preceding pages).

June 19, 1998
(Following pages) A view from above the almost complete stadium.

Baltimore not alone
on stadium overrun

AUGUST 1, 1997 — FOR MONTHS, MARYLAND STAdium Authority executive director Bruce Hoffman has issued a simple pledge so often it was beginning to sound like a mantra: The Ravens' stadium will open on time and on budget.

Until this week. With the announcement that the job will cost up to $20 million more than anticipated — due to a range of factors from team-requested extras to a spike in the cost of concrete — Hoffman joined a long list of stadium-builders called upon to explain embarrassing overruns.

From Cleveland to Phoenix, big-ticket sports complexes are running so far over budget that critics are wondering why anyone even bothered to budget in the first place.

March 20, 1998

Jerry Cook carries rebar for the bridge over light rail tracks. Concrete, like that about to be poured on this bridge, was a main reason for the overrun in stadium costs.

Consider: In Cleveland, the best bids to pour the new football stadium's concrete foundation and framing came in $15 million over the city's pre-bid estimate of $40 million. The bids were thrown out and the jobs re-configured, but concerns are mounting that the stadium may exceed the $247 million budget.

In Phoenix, wind tunnel tests revealed the design of the Bank One Ballpark now under construction needed more steel to keep the roof from blowing off. The result of this and other unexpected items: The ballpark for the baseball Diamondbacks has risen from $279 million to $350 million.

Experts cite a number of reasons for this stadium sticker shock, from the fast-track scheduling frequently demanded for sports arenas, which can require work to begin before all design work is completed, to last-minute changes demanded by team owners.

Also, the complexity of projects that involve thousands of workers and hundreds of subcontractors makes precision difficult. Something as simple as a wet spring or long winter can delay a project and require greater use of costly overtime.

Hoffman blamed a number of factors for the Ravens project going over its $200 million budget. The economy is running hotter than it was when Oriole Park came in on budget five years ago, he said. This creates more demand for everything from cement to stonemasons.

"Since 1989 to 1992, when we were building Oriole

Park, it's a much tougher contract," he said.

The biggest single item relates to the concrete used on the project. The stadium will use enough concrete to form a square column 100 feet wide and 16 stories tall. The state estimated it would cost $55 million, but ended up taking a bid for $70 million, Hoffman said.

The original budget for the Ravens' stadium called for $172 million for construction, $10 million to buy land for parking or to build a deck, $8 million for design work and $6.5 million for construction management, for a total of $196.5 million.

Hoffman now says the job will cost at least $10 million more and possibly $20 million more.

Mike Holleman, vice president of sports facilities for the Atlanta-based architectural firm of Heery International Inc., which is not involved in the Ravens job, said he's encountered similar problems.

"The whole construction industry is pretty busy. When everyone is busy, the contractors pick and choose what jobs they want to bid on and they don't bid as tight. There's no incentive to go out and cut your profit margins to be the low bidder," said Holleman, whose firm was involved in building the Olympic stadium now being used by the Braves.

Concrete prices too, have gone up substantially over the past few years, he said.

Despite these factors, Jack Kent Cooke Stadium, now being completed for the Redskins in the Landover area, has managed to stay within its $180 million budget, said project manager Walter Lynch. "Concrete came in pretty much on budget on our front," he said.

Operating as a private company enabled decisions to be made faster and costs to be more closely monitored, he said. And they faced fewer regulations and restrictions.

Maryland Stadium Authority chairman John Moag, however, said Baltimore's stadium will be better than the Redskins' — and worth the extra money.

"We're not going to build a Redskins stadium. We're going to build a top-quality stadium," Moag said. (To which Lynch replied: "The proof will be in the pudding.")

Kenneth Shropshire, an associate professor of legal studies and real estate at the University of Pennsylvania's Wharton School of Economics, said overruns on large, public works projects often seem worse than they are because of their scale.

The Ravens' stadium, for example, may be off by 10 percent — an amount a homeowner might consider reasonable for, say, a $2,000 room addition, he said.

Also, there are the complicating factors of politics. Community leaders may issue unreasonably low estimates in order to get a project approved.

"You've got the layers of contractors and subcontracts and the political layers," Shropshire said.

April 15, 1998
Supervisor Jim Indusi (right) and Joe Rodriguez check on plans for pavers on the north plaza area.

June 12, 1998
Ironworkers Joe Fousek (top) and John Edwards prepare railings for the main concourse.

July 8, 1997
*Ken Wheeler, Doug Buchanan and
Gregory Powell (left to right) set a
concrete form on top of columns.
Once in the place, the concrete will
support a decking platform.*

April 8, 1998
*Rodney Lynch sprays a coat of
primer on a wall at the club level.*

December 13, 1997
*(Following pages) Waterproofer
Conrad Acero caulks joints
between pieces of precast concrete
seating sections.*

Concrete achievement

AUGUST 10, 1997 — IT'S SHORTLY AFTER 8 A.M. AND several hundred workers are already swarming over the skeleton of the Ravens' stadium, clanging on iron bars, pumping concrete and hoisting steel girders with chugging, diesel cranes.

Into this maelstrom steps Alice Hoffman, the state's chief overseer of the $220 million project. Dressed in a peach, short-sleeved shirt, floral vest and brown slacks, she has traded her dress shoes for a pair of muddy boots. She also has put on a white hard hat and tinted safety glasses.

The weekly meeting of stadium contractors is in 40 minutes, and she wants to walk the site first and check on a few things.

A year has passed since work began on the job, and already it seems a lifetime. The Maryland Stadium Authority revealed recently that the project is now gobbling up cash at a rate $20 million over budget. This raised a chorus of "I told you so" from the legions of lawmakers and critics who view the stadium as a boondoggle.

August 6, 1997

Each morning, project manager Alice Hoffman makes the rounds of the stadium, checking on progress, looking for problems.

Opening day is still a year away, and it is Hoffman, project manager for the stadium, and a handful of others who will have the additional task of reining in the stampeding costs while still keeping the job on time.

A few minutes into her stadium tour, she finds a problem: A decorative veneer of concrete has been poured in a section of what will be the lower-deck concourse. Hoffman crouches down and plucks out a few tufts of plastic fiber, impregnated into the concrete for durability, and shakes her head. The fibers are OK, but missing are the thin grooves she ordered. She wanted these diagonal lines to radiate out a few feet from the four corners of each column, to reduce cracking at these stress points.

She makes a mental note to bring this up at the contractors' meeting.

It's not the first problem with concrete. The stadium authority blames the material, which will constitute about a third of the stadium's price tag, for much of its budget trouble. A surplus of construction jobs and shortage of workers in the raging economy has pushed up costs. Both the "precast" — the huge beams, slabs and terraced seating decks that are assembled like a jigsaw puzzle — and the "poured-in-place" concrete sections have soared in cost.

The state expected the concrete work to cost $55 million. It's now looking like $70 million. Design changes have also driven up costs, such as a decision to go with high-tech scoreboards and a multimillion-dollar sound system. The team will front the money for the extra work.

Shortly after 9 a.m., Hoffman is back in her construction trailer, under a Russell Street overpass, for the weekly progress meeting. Thirty-four people with radios, hard hats and clipboards crowd around a rectangular table in a conference room. They represent contractors and subcontractors specializing in bricklaying, waterproofing, plumbing and dozens of other specialties.

They are all men.

Hoffman is used to this. She is only 36, but has already held a variety of jobs in the male-dominated world of construction. A native of Granite City, Ill., she received a master's degree in civil engineering with a concentration in construction management from the Massachusetts Institute of Technology. From there, she got a job overseeing small projects in western Massachusetts for a New England telephone company, where she learned not to wear skirts on site visits to avoid gratuitous invitations to climb a ladder.

She took a job with a New Jersey bridge and tunnel maker, and made it to assistant project manager. Then she noticed there were no female project managers and didn't figure to be any soon. She left to join a quasi-public New York state developer of hospitals.

That's where she met stadium authority executive director Bruce Hoffman, who, despite sharing the same last name, is no relation. He was the boss of her boss at the New York agency and tried unsuccessfully, after coming to Baltimore, to draft her as project manager for Oriole Park.

She declined, for family reasons, but eventually ended up in Baltimore anyway, living on a sailboat at the Inner Harbor and consulting for Baltimore Systems Group.

Then the Cleveland Browns moved to Baltimore and became the Ravens. When Bruce Hoffman called this time, she said yes and moved back to the public sector, as a $90,000-a-year project director. She plans to go back to consulting when the stadium is complete.

The site's work force, now 750, is 99 percent male. Occasionally, she says, she has to "assert herself. It helps a lot that I'm in a position of authority. I control the checks."

At the 9 a.m. contractors meeting, Hoffman sits at the center of the table, next to Gary Harkness, who is the project manager for the construction management firm, a joint venture called Whiting Turner/Barton Malow/Essex. Harkness chairs the meeting, which lasts about an hour.

When they get to the concrete "topping" on the concourses, Hoffman notes the bothersome lack of diagonal grooves. After the meeting, she and a couple of contractors head for the architect's trailer to check the drawings.

It turns out the blueprints, used by the men who pour the concrete, were not updated to reflect her request for grooves. She is assured that will be done ASAP.

Back at her office, Hoffman tries to get some paperwork done. But the interruptions are constant. First, the project's quality control and inspection contractor stops by to report that some recently delivered steel beams are 2 inches too long. They've had other problems with this Canadian manufacturer, and Hoffman calls the company's president and sets up a visit to Montreal to discuss the issue the next week.

Moments later, there's a call from an oven manufacturer, who is on an airplane somewhere and worried he won't get a contract to equip the stadium's subterranean kitchens. He threatens to write the governor. Hoffman assures him his bid will get fair consideration.

Then architects from Kansas City are on the line, and Hoffman puts them on a speakerphone. The overruns have the stadium authority practicing "value engineering," otherwise known as the fine art of cutting out the fat. She wants to reduce the number of lights to be installed above some decorative ceiling panels, something that could save a lot of money. She has had a mock-up of this made and assures the Kansas City designers that it looks good.

She's also inquiring about deleting a big, steel canopy that was supposed to shield the skybox entrance to the stadium. Fabric would work just as well, she thinks. Thick, decorative steel bars on the stadium's exterior have already been replaced with thinner versions to save money.

The "tele-meeting" ends with the architects saying they have a committee going through the design looking for other ways to save money.

It's nearing lunchtime and Hoffman returns to the paperwork. She pores over a stack of last month's bills: $133,000 for ramp steel, $5,000 for security, $121,000 for paving, $2.8 million for precast concrete parts, $1.2 million for construction labor. She checks each one, signs it and sends it along to Bruce Hoffman.

After a quick lunch at an Indian restaurant in nearby Federal Hill, she is behind the wheel of her red Porsche 944 heading for Crownsville, outside Annapolis. The Chesapeake Bay Critical Areas Commission is meeting, and will be considering the stadium authority's plans for managing rainwater runoff on its parking lots.

The stadium authority wants to direct much of the water to a pair of small ponds south of the structure, as both a natural sewer and to meet its legal requirement to replace wetlands lost to construction.

Here, her day takes an-

June 19, 1997

In a work world dominated by men like these working on the lower deck, Alice Hoffman has moved through a variety of jobs.

Ravens' 'nest' takes shape

A bird's-eye view of the new stadium's progress

Ravens stadium is on schedule for completion by next year's preseason in August 1998.

The stadium is south of Oriole Park on 85 acres purchased and cleared in 1989 and 1990. Ravens stadium will be nearly twice as large as Oriole Park at 1.6 million square feet and 69,400 seats vs. the ballpark's 1 million square feet and 48,000 seats.

The football stadium will incorporate design innovations such as a discontiguous upper deck. This provides gaps at the corners so fans can see the cityscape outside, and allows the upper-deck sections at the end zones to be moved closer to the field.

Sightlines have been designed with the fan in mind. Front-row 50-yard-line seats in the lower deck will be 6 feet above the playing field and 50 feet from the sidelines. End-zone seats will start 20 feet from the end zone.

The stadium will have 70 bathrooms, 50 concession stands and more than 200 "points of sale" to buy food and drinks.

The exterior brick will be darker and richer than Oriole Park's to highlight the more industrial nature of Camden Yard's southern half.

Columns and beams of support

1 To form the playing field and lower seating area, a pit was dug to a depth of 25 feet below street level. It was in this area that fossil remains of an ancient bald cypress forest were found.

2 Steel pilings are driven into the ground at each point on the site where columns will be erected for support. They are hammered into the subsoil until a resistance of 4 inches of movement per six strikes of the pile driver is achieved. On this site, that pressure is realized at 50 feet.

3 Concrete is then poured around the pilings forming the caps on which steel "rebar" supports are set.

4 Forms, or molds, are then built on top of the caps and concrete is poured into them, forming the columns seen from street level.

5 Diagonal forms are built to top the columns, forming the beams on which seating will be placed.

6 Horizonal forms are then built and concrete is poured in to form cross beams.

7 Precast concrete decks, or floors, are placed and secured on top of the columns and beams.

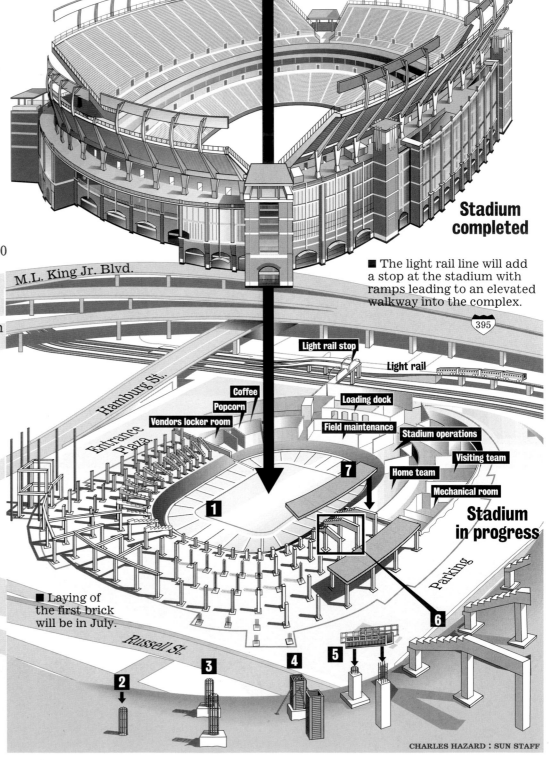

■ The grass field used at Memorial Stadium will be removed and reinstalled in the new stadium.

Stadium completed

■ The light rail line will add a stop at the stadium with ramps leading to an elevated walkway into the complex.

M.L. King Jr. Blvd.

395

Light rail stop

Light rail

Coffee

Popcorn

Vendors locker room

Loading dock

Field maintenance

Stadium operations

Visiting team

Home team

Mechanical room

Hamburg St.

Entrance Plaza

Parking

Stadium in progress

■ Laying of the first brick will be in July.

Russell St.

CHARLES HAZARD : SUN STAFF

122

other unexpected twist: Hoffman is on the schedule for 2:30 p.m. But the commission canceled a couple of items and ends up adjourning at 2 p.m., just as Hoffman arrives. She huddles with a few staffers and learns the plans have been approved, but the commission wants a sign put up near the ponds to educate people about the bay and water runoff.

Hoffman quickly agrees.

These meetings usually run hours longer, so Hoffman now finds unexpected time on her hands — a rare luxury. She lives nearby, having traded in her boat for a house, and decides against a return to the stadium. Instead, she tracks down a conference room in the building and launches into a pile of memos and paperwork.

She needs to prepare for tomorrow. There will be another weekly meeting, this one called the "owners meeting." As the chief representative of the stadium's owners — Maryland's taxpayers — she will chair this one. There will be no shortage of worries, from budgets to scoreboards, to discuss.

Not to mention those tiny grooves in the concrete.

"It's a lot of fun. It's different every day," she says of her job. "I think construction is one of the most complex endeavors undertaken by man."

August 6, 1997
With the complex matter of building a stadium to attend to, Hoffman faces new sets of challenges every day.

June 25, 1998
(Following pages) A light rail train passes under the pedestrian bridge.

New kid on the block

JULY 10, 1998 — WHEN THE PEOPLE DESIGNING Baltimore's new football stadium first gathered around the black marble conference table in the architect's offices Kansas City, Mo., two years ago, each brought a specific, and sometimes contradictory, vision of what the building should be.

For representatives of the Maryland Stadium Authority, the stadium had to mesh with Camden Yards' turn-of-the-century brick and mortar. For the Ravens, skyboxes and other money-making accouterments had to justify the move from Cleveland and to keep fans coming to games in an age when free broadcasts are as plentiful as beer commercials.

For the architects, HOK Sports Facilities Group, it was a chance to design the first publicly funded, all-football stadium in a decade. They wanted to define a new state of the art for a sport that has lagged badly behind baseball in stadium design.

But most of all, for everyone involved, the $220 million project had to live up to the toughest standard in sports: its graceful and much-acclaimed green cousin to the north, Oriole Park at Camden Yards.

"We had this incredible success that was sitting next to us which was hammered into us," said James Chibnall, HOK's lead designer of the Ravens project.

"Don't think that didn't keep me up at night thinking about that," he said.

Even though Ravens stadium will dwarf Oriole Park in size and cost, the quaint baseball park in many respects dominated the design of the new stadium.

That much was clear from that first meeting, where participants munched on Kansas City's renowned Gates barbecue and reviewed proposed designs.

Sitting at the table on the fifth floor of HOK's offices, a renovated, 100-year-old factory in Kansas City's old garment district, was Chibnall, now 37, an energetic senior project designer for the company. He made a splash with Jacobs Field in Cleveland, a forward-looking ballpark that opened in 1994 and reflected his view that merely recreating old-style buildings was not progress.

Bruce Hoffman was there, too. He is the executive director of the Maryland Stadium Authority and the man who guided Oriole Park to its acclaimed opening. A civil en-

February 26, 1998

Drywall finishers Steve Armstrong (left) and Luis Munoz work on the large window that faces downtown, just one of the design touches from HOK.

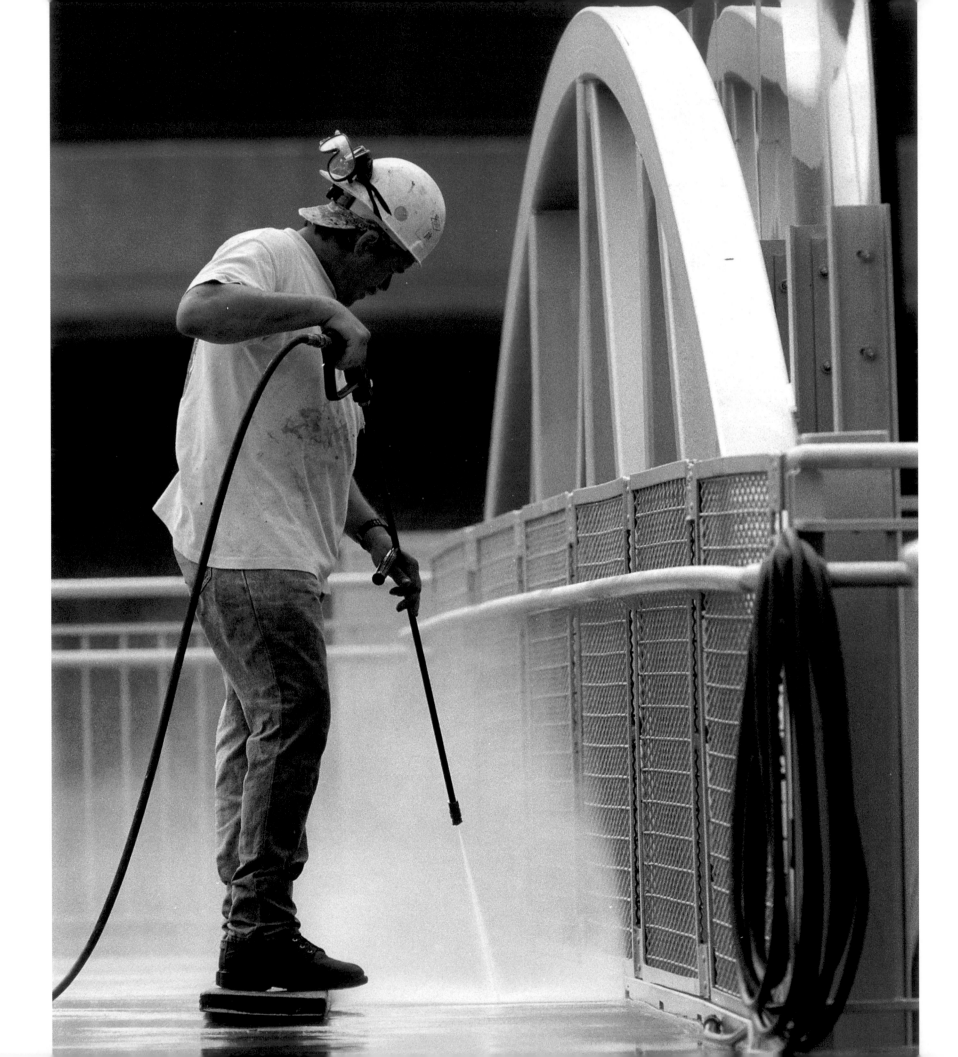

gineer who had previously overseen the construction of state hospitals and other projects for New York state, Hoffman, 50, had hit a home run with his first sports project and didn't want to strike out this time. He was intent on making the new stadium visually compatible with Oriole Park.

Representing team owner Art Modell at the meetings, and the entire design process, was James Bailey. Now 52, Bailey, buttoned-down and bespectacled, has been with Modell and the franchise for 20 years, first as a lawyer, then as in-house executive. He had been through countless failed efforts to wring a new stadium out of Cleveland and had very specific ideas about what a house for football should look like.

Also there were Ronald Labinski, 60, and Dennis Wellner, 48, two HOK founders who had guided the firm from its humble beginnings trying to scare up work around the country to its current status as the premier designer of athletic facilities worldwide. It is a status earned, in large measure, from the reception of Oriole Park.

Among them, the group had decades of experience in football and stadium design. But eight more months would be required to assemble all the elements for Baltimore.

Although free of the rancor that marked the development of Oriole Park, the process wasn't always smooth. There were disagreements along the way as opinions were melded into a design compromise that blends tradition with modernism, but will satisfy devotees of neither motif.

If the designers have succeeded, the new facility will change the way Americans view football games. Its signature will be its attempt to move beyond the utilitarian drudgery of most football buildings. Elements — chiefly its gap-toothed upper deck — have already been copied elsewhere. But whether the stadium will have the same revolutionary impact on its genre as Oriole Park did remains to be seen.

The stadium authority's Hoffman made it clear at the first meeting where he stood.

"It had to be brick, it had to have exposed steel and it had to have reinforced concrete. We wanted this to be a sports complex and to have compatibility" between Oriole Park and Ravens stadium, Hoffman recalled later.

That meant a brick facade and traditional feel — two elements that hadn't been seen much in football since the great college bowls of the 1920s. In fact, the designers reviewed books of old college stadiums for inspiration.

There was resistance to going too far with this. Some team officials and architects — who embraced the heretical view that Oriole Park's turn-of-the-century look was a tad unimaginative — favored a contemporary influence.

"What do we say when our children say, 'Why did they just build an old-looking stadium?' I don't know how to answer that," Chibnall said.

Football is a different sport, a newer sport, with its own history and aesthetic.

"The cultures of football and baseball demand different architecture. Baseball is a casual sport, played more frequently. Attending a football game is an event that consumes an entire day, beginning with the tailgating," Wellner said.

Initially, the designers considered a horseshoe-shaped stadium with the open end facing north — toward Oriole Park. This would resemble Memorial Stadium. In fact, the designers went to Memorial Stadium to look at how it worked.

The problem was the sun, which would always be in the eyes of the team receiving on the northern end. Also, eliminating one end zone of seating meant packing more seats in the remaining three sides. That would push them up and diminish the view of the uppermost ones.

By the time of the first meeting, the designers had decided to recommend — and the participants readily accepted — an east-west alignment of the park.

Other parameters were also set at the meeting.

Modell wasn't there, but he vowed to build the opposite of Cleveland's 80,000-seat Municipal Stadium — the oversized and outdated former home of the Browns and Indians — in Baltimore. He wanted an intimate park, with a capacity of less than 72,000, and one that featured broad concourses and the latest in boutique dining and posh corporate accommodations.

"My marching orders to my people were to make this so special that people would not want to stay home and watch it on TV," said Modell. "I have one philosophy: Today's no-show is tomorrow's no-buy."

He had the right, via the memorandum of agreement that brought the franchise to Baltimore, to veto its design.

Basic issues such as the number and style of locker rooms, video accommodations and press seating had all been thought out by the team over the years in Cleveland, where the team tried unsuccessfully to upgrade its stadium. Other matters, chiefly capacity and the number of luxury seats and suites, were quickly settled.

"We knew what we wanted. We didn't come in like farmers saying, 'Build us a stadium in a field,' " Modell said.

Hoffman was also intent on applying a few lessons from his experience with Oriole Park. For one thing, he hoped the new stadium would prove more adaptable and flexible. Spaces would be reserved for later expansion and remodeling.

"Oriole Park, as great as it is, is very, very tight. There is very little room to do anything," he said.

After the initial meeting, the participants went out for a tour of a few stadiums. They started with the Kansas City Chiefs' Arrowhead Stadium, the granddaddy of modern, single-purpose football stadiums. Then the group

June 25, 1998

Clyde Miller washes the bridge leading to the stadium light rail stop.

went on to two stadiums built for the NFL's most recent expansion teams: the Jacksonville Jaguars and Carolina Panthers.

"We got a chance to see different geometry and different ideas," Bailey said.

The team took the best of each, and rejected what it didn't like. The Carolina stadium's field, for example, is big enough for a World Cup soccer game. The Ravens, remembering the country mile that separated their fans and sidelines in Cleveland, rejected this in favor of keeping the seats as close to the sidelines as NFL rules allow.

And Jacksonville's pricey club seat section cuts a vertical swath from the field, between the 40-yard lines, up to the middle of the stadium. The Ravens talked about this arrangement but decided to go with a mezzanine level for club seats, similar to Charlotte and Oriole Park.

For its skyboxes, the team opted for a stacked arrangement of two tiers, with none in the end zones. This keeps the suites along the sidelines where they can attract the highest rent.

With these basic decisions made, construction got under way, based on an outline still being filled in by designers. Gradually, through a series of interlocking decisions, the form took shape.

To accommodate the 108 skyboxes the team wanted, the press level had to be bumped down, below the club seat deck, displacing some lower-deck seats and pushing the upper deck higher.

Quite by accident, this also led to the most dramatic architectural innovation in the stadium, its notched upper-deck corners.

While tinkering with the deck design, Chibnall realized that the skyboxes and club seats and press level were pushing the upper deck up along the sidelines. But this didn't mean the end zones had to rise with it.

So he set them free.

He broke the upper deck into four pieces, long sections along the sidelines and shorter ones overlooking each end

July 13, 1998
A skybox patron can take this spiral path down to a lower level.

zone. He then pushed down in the end-zone sections. This moved these seats closer to the field, improving the sight-lines for what are typically the toughest tickets to sell.

It was an inspired notion and, perhaps more than any-thing else, created the signature by which Ravens stadi-um will be remembered. Already, stadiums in Cleveland and Cincinnati have adopted variations of the theme.

A major refinement of the idea was offered by Labin-ski, HOK's spiritual leader, whose office is denoted by a sign identifying him as the "grey eminence." He was look-ing over Chibnall's shoulder one day while the designer was sketching ideas on tissue paper (Chibnall often does creative work on a drawing board, rather than the com-puters favored by many colleagues).

Labinski asked: Why not shave off the corners of the four upper-deck pieces to open up the stadium?

He then wandered off.

"One of the unique things about Ron is he's always will-ing to offer an idea and walk away and let it flower in the designer," Chibnall said.

The effect broke the old rules of football stadium design. No longer would the fans be confined to a concrete oval walled off from the outer world. Now people on the in-side would be able to glimpse the urban skyscape around them and passers-by would be able to peek inside.

In a sense, the football stadium would now gain the sort of integration with its surrounding community, or "transparency," that is the hallmark of Oriole Park.

"If you're coming north on Russell Street, you can look right into the upper deck. That's the kind of thing archi-tects drool over," said Steve Evans, HOK's project man-ager on the job.

It simultaneously solved a number of problems. It brought the capacity of the stadium down to what the team wanted, by eliminating unpopular corner seats. It broke up the crown of the building, making it appear smaller, as Hoffman wanted.

Later, the designers tried another unorthodox ap-proach, this time with the pedestrian ramps that will lead the fans to the upper concourses.

Traditional football stadium design exaggerates the visual impact of these elevated sidewalks, resulting in a building that looks like a parking garage. At Ravens stadi-um, the designers kept the ramps inside the exterior brick walls. Fans will enter the building through one of the arch-ways and then head up.

"We wanted there to be a psychological sense of arriv-ing in a building. A front door. You are not arriving at a ramp. The building has a sense of grandeur. You go into this building before you begin your climb," Chibnall said.

Early drawings called for pedestrian ramps at each corner. But this was dropped late in the process in favor of a different alignment: one ramp in each of the northern corners, and two overlapping on the center of the south face. In essence, there are three "stairwells."

Using three ramp areas breaks up the symmetry and gives the club lounge on the north side of the stadium, be-tween the ramps, a wide view of Oriole Park and the down-town skyline beyond. On the south side, the lounges were pushed to the corners, giving them views of the Middle Branch of the Patapsco River and south Baltimore in-stead of a homely warehouse.

The exterior was the subject of much negotiation. Hoffman, representing the traditionalists, sought to max-imize the brick and its traditional feel, but wanted to keep the building's scale down. Heidi Edwards, an architect

July 13, 1998

Details, details. Derek Puffenbarger of The Marble Source Unlimited touches up a coffee table in a skybox.

hired by the Ravens, wasn't troubled by the size and argued for extending the brick all the way up the stadium, using brick-framed windows instead of a contemporary-looking wall of sheer glass.

"We want the place to seem big because it is big," Edwards said.

Chibnall tugged toward a more modernistic appearance in keeping with football's relative youth as a major-league sport. He pushed for more glass on the exterior, to break up the scale.

"We came to the compromise of having the brick at the base and skinned it with a curtain wall of glass above it," Chibnall said.

"Our desire was to create this massive base and as your eye went up make it more abstract and blend in with the sky," he said.

How will the stadium be received?

On this the people who met that first day in Kansas City disagree. The designers think it will be influential, but probably not as revolutionary as Oriole Park.

Hoffman says its enduring contribution will be the attempt to dress up the exterior — contrary to most football stadiums, even those recently opened — and blend it in with an urban landscape.

"What could come out of this is a football stadium that is woven into the community and is pretty," he said.

Said Evans, who oversaw both stadiums: "I don't think any one project will have the effect of Oriole Park. I don't think you'll see Ravens stadium as an icon. I believe the Camden Yards complex will be an icon."

Chibnall said: "I think it will be very well-received as a building. It's almost unfortunate that it had to compete with Oriole Park. They are totally different buildings and two totally different sports."

June 19, 1998
Greetings, Earthlings. It may look like a flying saucer, but this device, sitting atop a light tower, is supposed to help protect from lightning strikes inside the stadium.

August 26, 1997
(Following pages) Even at the midpoint of construction, workers remained on the job even after the sun had set.

Builders pit game plan against clock at stadium

JUNE 15, 1998 — THE BATTLE BEGINS ANEW EACH morning, as the sun peeks over the horizon, casting its light on a pockmarked terrain of rubble, machines and spent iron.

Here, hundreds of men and women mass with battered helmets on their heads, goggles dangling from their necks. In their hands are the weapons of their trades: drills, saws, hammers and torches.

They are in the final, frenzied two months of a battle with a rigorous deadline. They will have gone from drawing board to football stadium in two years and two months. The outer shell is nearly complete, the electricity and plumbing all working. But there is still much to be done before kickoff Aug. 8.

This is no time to let up.

Such has it been from the start. Amid clanging steel and choking dirt, the workers have thrown themselves each day at the task of constructing an elegant stadium of green glass and

April 8, 1998

The race to finish the stadium can't mean overlooking details. Ray McGaha (left) and Mike Henshaw are headed to the top of a scoreboard to seal its edges.

red brick on what used to be a parking lot south of Oriole Park at Camden Yards.

They are architects and excavators and carpenters and crane operators and pipe fitters. They come from union hiring halls and corporate offices. Working with materials as soft as putty and as hard as brick, they give three-dimensional life to a set of blueprints as big as a coffee table.

The job is a high-profile one, literally and figuratively. The stadium is about as tall and long as the Titanic and five times as wide. One of the most prominent features on the city's skyline, it is the first thing thousands of commuters and tourists see as they arrive downtown every day.

Any shortcomings are sure to be attacked by fans and an unforgiving media, not to mention taxpayers who are paying the bulk of the stadium's $222 million cost. Conversely, if it succeeds, the stadium could define a new state of the art, just as Oriole Park did for baseball.

This is no simple barn raising. By the time the 69,000-seat stadium opens, more than 200,000 tons of concrete will have been poured and formed, 16 miles of handrails galvanized and installed and more than a million bricks cemented into place.

Steel piles will have been jammed nearly 90 feet into

bedrock and delicate light bulbs installed 165 feet in the air.

A jail, weight room and X-ray center will have opened in the basement.

Six hundred forty-seven public toilets and 321 urinals will have been installed and tested in 72 bathrooms. More than a million feet of electrical wiring will have been strung, creating a network capable of handling enough juice to power five buildings the size of Baltimore's World Trade Center.

And it absolutely, positively must be done by Aug. 8, when the Chicago Bears come to town for a preseason game.

Vincent Keim, a foreman supervising the installation of railings on the upper deck a few weeks ago, felt the pressure. And he passed it on down, hustling back and forth between crews under his watch like Stonewall Jackson inspecting his battle lines on horseback.

"It's pretty hard. I'm trying to infect the people with urgency," Keim said between exchanges on a scuffed-up walkie-talkie.

Behind and below him was the muddy dirt that would eventually be a football field. In front of him were the tiered rows of white concrete, about half-filled with purple seats. As he watched workers bolt pewter-colored railings to one corner of the concrete seating bowl, others from a completed section suggested moving on. Keim refused. He wanted all available hands completing each section before going on to the next, doing the job right so nothing has to be redone.

"Just knowing that it's a stadium and that so many people are going to come and see it makes it tougher. It's got to look pretty," Keim said.

Nearly 700 people are on the site, the final regiments of a transitory army of 3,000 that will have worked on the project over the past two years. They come in waves depending on their specialties, completing their tours of duty and turning over the work to fresh recruits.

"It's a coming-and-going effect. It's not like anybody's been here from the beginning," said Alice Hoffman, the Maryland Stadium Authority's project manager on the job.

Except her, of course. The 37-year-old, Porsche-driving civil engineer from southern Illinois has experience building bridges, tunnels and buildings. But this is her first stadium.

She is the field marshal, working out of a cluttered trailer under the Russell Street overpass, pushing the project along. A sign on her office door reads: "Shut up and Build."

"You have plans and contingencies and fallbacks. You have a common goal, and everybody knows what it is," Hoffman said. "And you have a common enemy: time and money."

So far, money has the upper hand. The budget has been busted by higher-than-anticipated concrete costs

blamed, in part, on poor productivity by the contractor, Clark Construction Group. A job that started out costing $200 million will likely hit $222 million. The team has kicked in some cash, and frills have been cut to keep the costs from going any higher.

The state still believes it will deliver the stadium on time. Doing so requires manpower. Lots of it. The job has hit two employment peaks of about 1,000 each, once when the concrete work was at its zenith and another about two months ago when the finishing work was at its height.

Such a payroll is costly: Wages range from $9.80 an hour for laborers pushing brooms to $21.50 for skilled electricians.

There's not a lot of socializing on the site. The work is demanding and the pace brisk. Friends may exchange greetings at the gates before or after work or during safety meetings. But the breaks are short.

"They are really pushing this one. Everything is on a rush-type basis," said Mark Robinson, a 27-year-old caulker from Clinton busy sealing gaps on the stadium's northern club level, a glassed-in lounge area with a panoramic view of downtown.

Down in the basement, Craig Wagner, a 38-year-old, self-employed cabinetmaker, was installing counter tops in a windowless trainer's room. For months, he rose at 4:45 each morning at his home in Fulton to make it to the stadium at 6:30 a.m. But he's seen only the parts of the giant stadium where he is working.

"I never have walked around the place," Wagner said.

About half the stadium workers are on a six-day schedule. Sundays are normally quiet, although it's not uncommon to find a few craftsmen on the job.

The first shifts begin at 5:30 a.m. or 6:30 a.m. A short morning break comes at 9 a.m. Lunch is a half-hour, and although the machinery falls silent, most of the workers pull out lunch boxes wherever they happen to be, eating with their work crew. There's no cafeteria or water cooler for congregating. The first of the shifts ends at 2:30 p.m.

Then a second-shift crew comes in, usually doing work such as heavy lifting with cranes that is best accomplished with a minimum of people on the site. Sometimes there has been a third shift as well, keeping the site alive around the clock.

Having so many people doing so many things in such close quarters inevitably creates friction. Occasionally, a worker will steal another's tools or vandalize his work. Fights break out.

Tension between union and nonunion workers simmers. Wagner, the carpenter, said co-workers have been friendly enough, but he has seen derogatory

March 20, 1998

Painting, such as that being done by Osvaldo Alvarez, sometimes has to be repeated because of the nature of construction work.

graffiti inside a portable toilet about nonunion workers such as himself.

"There's union and nonunion people on the job," Wagner said. "If you're in a union, you're pro-union. If you're not, you don't really care one way or the other."

It's not just a matter of money. Maryland law requires the stadium authority to pay prevailing wages, but didn't insist on union workers as some other states have. This angers unionists, who see their once-solid grip on jobs like this slipping away.

Bud Culp, a 60-year-old carpenter working a waterproofing detail on a few months ago, for example.

He wore drab green work pants, a mustard-yellow canvas vest and the scraggly white beard of a mariner. His hard hat had a "Proud to be Union" decal. The son of a Western Maryland coal miner, Culp has worked construction for 30 years. He plans to retire once the stadium is finished.

"They say it's a union job, but you get down here and it's half nonunion. My dad was a union coal miner. They don't fool around with that stuff like this," Culp said.

Pickets have gone up twice — once last year when the AFL-CIO was protesting the paucity of unionized workers at the site and in March, when a handful of drywallers charged their nonunion employer with transferring them out of state when it found the men were union members.

The stadium authority estimates that unionized contractors have gotten about $158 million worth of contracts. And Maryland-based contractors have received $144 million worth of work, the state says.

Whatever their differences, workers on the project have to watch each other's backs. Distractions, inattention or just bad luck can have disastrous results.

In October, ironworker David Scheper was working on the southern stairwell when he took a wrong step and fell 13 feet onto a sheet of corrugated steel.

"I made a big crater," Scheper said.

He landed on his back, with his right arm twisted behind him. It snapped in two places, leaving a bone sticking out above his elbow and his wrist bent in an unnatural, 90-degree angle.

"It didn't hurt that much at the time. But an hour later, when I was at the hospital and they reset it, it really hurt," Scheper said.

Just 10 days earlier, another man had broken both legs in a 25-foot fall from nearly the same place.

Colleagues began whispering about ghosts haunting the unlucky stairwell. It became know as the Indian burial ground.

September 26, 1997

The structural steel comes together in the upper reaches of the stadium.

In November 1996, another worker nearly lost his foot. He was working on a crew pounding pilings 16 inches in diameter into the ground. Standing 60 feet up a ladder, he was maneuvering the heavy pile driver when a hydraulic system gave out and the pile driver crushed his foot against a piling.

The injured man was taken to the Maryland Shock Trauma Center, just up the street. Surgeons managed to reattach his toes, but he missed six months of work. The Ravens sent players to visit him in the hospital. Co-workers took up a collection.

At the outset, the stadium authority hired a full-time safety director for the project, to augment the safety representatives each contractor is required to employ. He convenes weekly meetings and walks the site armed with a digital camera. When he sees a hazard, he photographs it, stops it and sends the picture along with a fine to the contractor.

Fines range from $50 to $1,000, said Jeff Provenzano, the safety director. He can also fire a worker for acting dangerously.

"A lot of these guys are working long hours, seven days a week. There's a lot of stress," he said.

As do all good commanders, the stadium authority takes steps to keep morale up, to build "unit cohesion" despite the ever-present pressure and danger.

The authority and some of the large contractors occasionally provide a catered meal. There was a Fourth of July cookout, a Labor Day picnic, Thanksgiving lunch and a hot breakfast for Christmas.

On Valentine's Day this year, Hoffman had a few hundred cakes baked and handed them out at the gate as workers left that Saturday. One of the men, who was working his last day before a planned retirement, took it home to his wife and died the next day of a heart attack.

At times like that, construction workers have a tradition of passing a hat for the family. On the Ravens job, hats have been passed for serious injuries, deaths in the family and even one visitor.

Stephen, a 5-year-old boy dying of a brain tumor, showed up on the site in 1996 as the ground rumbled with bulldozers and excavators. Through a grant-a-wish organization, Stephen had asked to see a working construction project.

He came on a Saturday, arriving in a donated limousine, and touched the hearts of the workers. On his head, left hairless by medical treatment, was a Ravens cap and a tiny hard hat. He spent several hours on the site, sitting on the laps of workers as they drove trucks and 'dozers. He went home with a toy crane.

He died six days later. His grandfather called Hoffman to say the boy spoke often of his visit to the Ravens site. Workers passed a hat on the anniversary of his death to send the family money.

To an outsider, the stadium looks like barely contained chaos. The broad concourses, which will one day be

full of fans munching cheeseburgers and sipping micro-brews, are cluttered with lift trucks and strewn with debris. There are boxes of seat brackets, bundles of bricks and empty buckets of drywall mud.

There is even wildlife. Sea gulls appear like clockwork during the lunch hour, hoping to scoop up a dropped french fry. And, each morning, a flock of large, black birds takes up position on the uppermost section of the project. They are most likely crows, but the workers kid about their being ravens, there to check the progress.

"It's like they are watching it," Hoffman said.

In general, the stadium is being built from east to west, from bottom to top.

"We're trying to be very efficient," said Heidi Edwards, a Washington-based architect hired as project manager for the Ravens at the suggestion of Janet Marie Smith, the former Orioles consultant who played a similar role at Camden Yards.

"We have to sequence things so we have a natural progression," said Edwards, 33.

When this progression breaks down, painters overtake the drywallers, or the people bolting the seats to the brackets catch up with the workers bolting brackets to the concrete seating decks. This sets off a ripple of delays that can run around the stadium. Soon, craftsmen are standing around idle for $25 an hour.

Supervisors — "white hats" in construction lingo, so known because of their white hard hats — hustle to change directions, start a new project, or otherwise accommodate the new hurdle.

"The object is to never stop work," Edwards says.

For example, Waverly Rawlings and his partner, Dante Kelly, were the vanguard of a painting crew that started in the first skybox on the stadium's northwest corner and worked its way clockwise around the oval.

First Rawlings and Kelly come through, armed with pneumatic sprayers and rollers, to prime the walls. A few doors down, another crew followed with the yellow top-coat — two shades, one for the bulkheads around the windows and a darker hue for the walls.

Behind them were finishers and woodworkers, installing the dark-wood-veneered cabinets and marble counter tops. Then came ceiling and lighting specialists and carpet installers.

There is constant pressure to keep up.

"It's a big job, but they seem to be on top of it. Everybody knows their job and does it," said Rawlings, 32, of Solomon's Island.

July 13, 1998

Mark Parker touches up the wood stain on cubicles in the Ravens locker room.

Sometimes other craftsmen will nick the paint while installing cabinets or lights or ceiling tiles. A touch-up crew will have to dab these spots later. This is frustrating, but a part of construction.

Rawlings said he has found this job better coordinated than his last, the Redskins stadium at Landover. There have been fewer of the mix-ups that raise tempers and force work to be redone, Rawlings said. The Redskins stadium was built in 18 months. Baltimore's is on a relatively leisurely 26-month pace. (Oriole Park took 28.)

But even that figure is deceiving. Stadiums are unlike most other construction jobs, where designers and architects draw up plans and hand them over to contractors for execution. Projects such as the Ravens stadium are generally conducted on a "fast-track" system in which work gets under way before the design is completed. In the case of the Baltimore project, architects in Kansas City were less than two months into the job when ground was broken at Camden Yards on July 23, 1996.

They decided early in the process how the stadium would be oriented — with the 50-yard line running just off a north-south axis — and about how large its exterior would be. That meant the excavators could start in August 1996, digging a hole 900 feet long, 800 feet wide and 18 feet deep.

Then, workers established a point of reference, a ground zero from which everything else would be measured and located. The stadium's "work point," as it is known, is a chunk of concrete about as big as a manhole cover. It is where the 50-yard line will be, precisely where the referee will flip the coin to decide who kicks and who receives (the work point at Oriole Park was home plate).

By the time this was completed, the designers knew enough about what the superstructure would look like that they could say with precision where columns would need to be built.

While designers fleshed out details of the stadium's interior, contractors went to work sinking legs in the ground to give the stadium secure footing. A total of 3,600 pilings were driven into the ground by a massive pile driver. Workers knew they had gone deep enough when each whack of the driver knocked a piling only 6 inches deeper.

Sometimes a piling reached this point 25 feet down. Sometimes, in looser muck, one might go nearly 90 feet. The piles were then pumped full of slurpy concrete and a platform was built around them, from which the stadium would rise.

Then it was upward and onward.

Workers built hundreds of concrete columns, each as wide as a sidewalk. These were connected by concrete beams prefabricated at a factory in Virginia, which were topped by prefabricated slabs or corrugated steel to form the concourses and seating bowls. The effect was not unlike a jigsaw puzzle being assembled.

Walls were crafted under the stands out of cinder blocks and an exterior facing of red brick, mined from Potomac River clay in Western Maryland, was assembled one at a time. Glass went up on the exterior, the heat was turned on and drywallers, carpenters, painters and plumbers moved in to complete the inner portions.

In the meantime, designers for subcontractors worked out details of the stadium's complicated plumbing, electrical and ventilation systems. They couldn't start until the master plan was far enough along to determine how much electricity and water would be needed and where.

As the stadium's form took shape, unanticipated gaps and problems came into view. For example, Hoffman was walking through the place a few months ago, examining the concession stands being built, when she noticed something missing: the 4-inch plastic strip, familiar to home kitchen remodelers, that goes around the base of the wall.

"I went back to my office and looked it up on the plans, and it wasn't there. No one had thought of it," Hoffman said. It had to be added.

For all the work that has been accomplished, much remains to be done. The club lounges are being decorated. The earth surrounding the site is being bulldozed smooth for landscaping and a whimsical "X's and O's" pattern laid in tile around the north entrance. Installers are finishing the seats, a painstaking job. Installation of the hybrid grass and plastic field — really a relocation from Memorial Stadium — is under way.

The deadline is looming.

"One of my bosses is running around like a chicken with his head cut off," said Robinson, the caulker.

As workers complete a part of the job, they turn it over to the final phase — inspection and correction. The plan calls for all of July to be devoted to this remedial work, called "punching out."

The first wave of July's inspection will come from the architects, who will walk through completed sections drawing up a "punch list" of errors or problems. Next, team and state officials will walk through, going over the list and adding their own items.

No matter is too small for inclusion: a cracked light switch here, a smudged wall there. In coming months, teams will have the laborious job of inspecting each of the 69,000 seats, one at a time, making a note of each one that squeaks, sags or otherwise malfunctions.

Government inspectors, too, have their say. Health officials recently demanded $75,000 worth of additional caulking to the concession stands.

The lists are then turned over to the construction manager, who assigns each item to the contractor responsible. Workers go back in to do the repairs, checking off each item and initialing it on the punch list.

It is detailed, complicated work that can spark confrontations among contractors who blame one another for errors and try to avoid paying for the repairs.

Plenty can still go wrong, but Hoffman is growing confident that the war against the clock will be won.

"Unless we get a fire or tornado or something, we'll be open," she said. "I'm feeling pretty good about it."

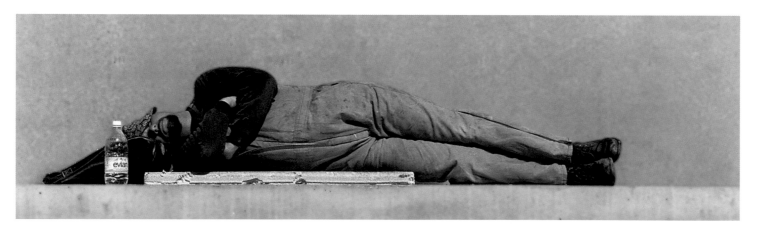

February 26, 1998
On an unseasonably warm day, plumber Darryl Anderson rests during his lunch hour.

August 5, 1997
Two masons build a bathroom wall on the main concourse.

144

September 26, 1997
*Even at their accelerated pace,
workers do need to take breaks
for some things.*

August 5, 1997
*Heaven or hell? Workers who
use this ladder obviously are of
two minds.*

147

Epilogue

TIME WILL TELL IF THE STADIUM THAT BURST from the ground at Camden Yards in 1997 and 1998 will live up to the standards set by its neighbor to the north, Oriole Park. But in a financial sense, the impact is undeniably lucrative for the team — as it was for the Orioles.

The Ravens' 108 skyboxes were nearly fully leased by opening day, other than those withheld for the owner and VIPs, sell for $55,000 to $200,000 a season and produce about $10 million in revenue each year for the team. The 7,900 club seats, also sold out, were bringing in another $15 million or so — windfalls teams in older stadiums can only dream about.

As was typical for new stadiums, the ticket prices reflected an expectation of high demand. They averaged $40.37 a game, not including the premium seats. This would generate, after deductions for the visiting team, about $15 million a season assuming near-sellouts. That doesn't include the "permanent seat licenses" required of season-ticket holders. The one-time fee ranged from $200 for an upper-deck corner seat to $3,000 on the 50-yard-line.

June 20, 1998

Looking west into a sunset, a nearly finished stadium awaits players at Camden Yards.

Concessions, corporate tent rentals on the parking lots, stadium advertising and a naming-rights deal promised to bring in many more millions of dollars. No wonder, then, the league felt comfortable enough with the team's financial projections to allow it to borrow $185 million in 1997.

This was well in excess of the league's ordinary borrowing limits, and was achieved with a sleight of hand: NFL rules limit how much debt a team's managing partner can take on using the franchise as collateral. But the rules don't apply to co-investors. So, in late 1997, Art Modell transferred 70 percent of the team's stock, though not operational control, to his wife of 28 years, Pat. She became the owner.

Coupled with a network television deal that would pay each team $73 million a year into the next century, the franchise that Art Modell bought for less than $4 million in 1961 was now quite possibly worth 100 times that amount.

In baseball, the infusions of cash from new stadiums has resuscitated old franchises and turned upside down old assumptions about big markets versus small markets. The same was inevitable in football. Properly managed, a team with a stadium and revenues like the Ravens had to be a threat on the field.

What, then, would the community gain? The NFL was back in town, to the relief and celebration of many. The Camden Yards complex was now complete, fulfilling a commitment made by state lawmakers in 1986.

The costs proved higher than anyone guessed: about $500 million for the twin stadiums.

In terms of economic development, the state estimated hundreds of jobs and millions of dollars would flow to the public. But independent economists are nearly unanimous in disputing those projections.

Many say such high-priced projects are, in fact, break-even or even losing propositions financially for their communities. Teams such as the Ravens merely redirect leisure spending that would likely take place anyway in the community, in essence robbing Peter to pay Paul.

Meanwhile, other needs, from schools to smaller-scale economic development opportunities, go unmet.

But at least Baltimore, a city that had spent much of its sports history buffeted by greedy owners and forces beyond its borders, was now setting the standard for other cities to live up to — a gold standard.

The Ravens stadium would be remembered for its attention to the extras, for going beyond the austere design that had up until then been the norm in football stadiums.

Its exterior, designed to complement Oriole Park, contained more than 1 million bricks. Oversized, pewter-colored beams lent a gritty, industrial look meant to conjure up visions of Baltimore's steelmaking, shipbuilding heydays.

The segmented upper deck gave fans on the inside a view of downtown and the surrounding community that was growing common in baseball but was revolutionary for football.

There were grumbles, too, though: The building was an immense intrusion into the skyscape, dwarfing Oriole Park and jarring commuters accustomed to the baseball park's more gentle visual introduction to the city.

The upper deck was also very high, pushed up by the double-decked skyboxes and club level.

But the team promised a fan experience that it hoped would override all those other concerns. It sent much of the stadium staff to Disney World to learn how to treat customers. A $10 million audio-visual system, operated by a team schooled in rock concerts and movie making, promised to change old assumptions about the role of video entertainment at sporting events.

Ultimately, no amount of technology or image making or bricks can create a bond between athletes and a city. Whether the stadium succeeds or not will be determined by the fans in the years to come.

July 15, 1998
Bob Bennett instructs participants in how proceed with the "super flush," which simulates halftime bathroom usage.

July 15, 1998
Welder Tim Smith installs a security gate near an entrance on the southwestern side of the stadium.

December 19, 1996

May 22, 1997

December 13, 1997

February 26, 1998

June 19, 1997

September 26, 1997

April 8, 1998

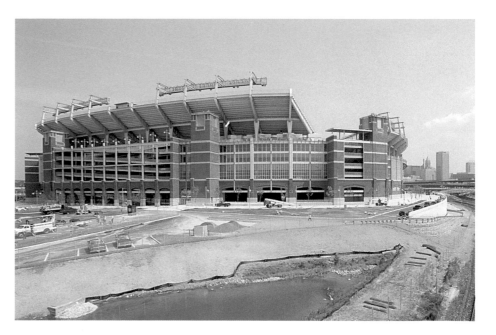

July 21, 1998

June 9, 1997
A brick bearing the team's name stands ready to be set during a "first brick" ceremony.

August 8, 1998
(Preceding pages) The completed project in its natural state: the Ravens take on the Bears in the stadium's first preseason game.

Stadium by the numbers

Miles of handrails 16

Miles of reinforcing steel in block walls 58

Miles of wire reinforcement in block walls 82

Feet of height for tower cranes 250

Steel piles under the stadium 3,600

Pieces of structural precast concrete 4,000

Football players to equal the weight of mortar holding stadium bricks together 13,866

Pounds that tower cranes can lift 44,000

Pounds in some beams supporting the upper seating bowl 70,000

Pounds of bricks and mortar laid by each bricklayer 450,000

Pounds of block and mortar laid by each block layer ....1.1 million

Bricks in the stadium ....1.2 million

Pounds of precast concrete ....134 million

Pounds of cast-in-place concrete ....240 million

Other Books from The Baltimore Sun:

Cal Touches Home

Motherhood Is A Contact Sport

The Wild Side of Maryland: An Outdoor Guide

The 1996-1997 Maryland Business Almanac

Raising Kids and Tomatoes *(forthcoming)*

The Great Game of Maryland Politics *(forthcoming)*

This *Sun* book was published by SunSource, an information service of *The Sun*. To order any of the above titles, or for information on research, reprints and information from the paper's archives, please call 410.332.6800.